T0380273

REMOTELY CLOSE

A Practical Guidebook for Christian Online Higher Education

DR. DANIEL R. DAY

WESTBOW
PRESS®
A DIVISION OF THOMAS NELSON
& ZONDERVAN

WestBow Press books may be ordered through booksellers or by contacting:

WestBow Press
A Division of Thomas Nelson & Zondervan
1663 Liberty Drive
Bloomington, IN 47403
www.westbowpress.com
844-714-3454

ISBN: 979-8-3850-2226-7 (sc)
ISBN: 979-8-3850-2225-0 (hc)
ISBN: 979-8-3850-2244-1 (e)

Library of Congress Control Number: 2024906223

Print information available on the last page.

WestBow Press rev. date: 04/30/2024

DEDICATION

To Sara, my bride and the love of my life.
To my daughter, MJ, and my son, Jonathan.
Most of all, to my Savior and Lord, Jesus Christ.

PRAISE FOR REMOTELY CLOSE

This book is a homerun! A veritable Spring-Training for every online educator in America today!

David & Jason Benham
Acclaimed Entrepreneurs, Authors, Speakers, Former MLB Baseball Players

As believers navigating the digital realm, Dr. Day offers invaluable insights and strategies to foster spiritual growth alongside academic excellence. Remotely Close will help anyone seeking to integrate faith into their online learning journey.

Sam Rodriguez
Best-selling Author, Film Producer, & Lead Pastor
President of the National Hispanic Christian Leadership Conference

This book is a crucial resource for any Christian College or University. Dr. Day's practical and engaging writing style brings this relevant study to life.

Dr. Kent Ingle
President of Southeastern University

Remotely Close is the 'How to Win Friends and Influence People' of online education...A must read for everyone looking to improve online student engagement and professional satisfaction.

Scott Wilson
Author, Pastor, and
President of Ready, Set, Grow

I commend Dr. Day's efforts to provide current data that interfaces with the larger theological questions that should be placed before anyone whose vocation is to develop Spirit-empowered leaders for the 21st-century Church.

Dr. Byron Klaus
Board of Directors at In Trust Center for Theological Schools
Co-Editor of The Globalization of Pentecostalism
Past President of the Assemblies of God Theological Seminary

Dr. Daniel Day's Remotely Close is a comprehensive and invaluable resource for educators navigating the realm of online learning within a Christian context. With clarity and insight, Dr. Day offers practical strategies and thoughtful guidance for integrating online educational principles and practices into the digital classroom. This book is a must-read for anyone seeking to foster meaningful connections, uphold values, and deliver quality education in the increasingly remote landscape of higher education.

Dr. Mark Hausfeld
Author, Professor, Missionary
Past President of the Assemblies of God Theological Seminary

Daniel's book is a recipe for successful Christian online education. The perfect mix of practical insight and high-level research.

Anne F. Beiler
Auntie Anne's Pretzel Company, Founder

I hope that the "Remotely Close" classroom becomes the default posture of Christian online educational delivery systems.

Dr. Earl Creps
Author & Professor

The ability to create community, establish a culture, and engage in relationships will separate schools that do online education well from those that do not. Dr. Day offers practical insight and research-based evidence on how an online institution can accomplish these tasks while remaining academically strong and true to the institution's values. The research and methodology presented will help one make their online educational program both engaging and life-giving for the student, the faculty, and the institution. Dr. Day is a proven leader in this field, and this book will reflect his understanding of and passion for online education.

Dr. Andrew Templeton
Director of Online Education
Northpoint Bible College and Seminary

Poorly designed and executed online programs rob students of an essential element of education: relationships. Dr. Daniel Day's Remotely Close provides proven and effective solutions to allow students and instructors to have a dynamically relational learning experiences even when not physically close.

Dr. Alan Ehler
Lead Pastor, Professor, and Former Academic Dean

Dr. Daniel Day's work on remote learning comes at exactly the right moment in Church history. With the Great (Pastoral) Resignation now emptying pulpits across the nation, online ministry training becomes a critical tool for restoring the strength of America's churches. I highly recommend it!

Dr. Bill Hennessy
Lead Pastor Life360 All Nations
Life360 Executive Director of Operations
Online Educator

Remotely Close provides valuable insight into the challenges and experiences of online education. This book reveals the crucial role of social integration in ensuring academic success and satisfaction in online learning for both students and professors. It is essential reading for anyone navigating the world of virtual education.

Dr. Meredith James
Ministry Leadership Educator

TABLE OF CONTENTS

FOREWORD

By: Dr. Byron Klaus

Higher education has been undergoing a huge change in basic assumptions over the last decade. Among the multiple factors that reflect this changing landscape is the advance of learning management systems to facilitate online learning. Additionally, the group historically called the *non-traditional student* has become a majority of all students in post-secondary education. The saga of the COVID-19 era only revealed those realities and subsequent challenges exponentially. If the hope were to return to a more secure and stable era that preceded the COVID-19 experience, we soon realized that the picture of stability was overrated. Even more daunting, it was not documentable.

The issues of affordability and accessibility have been the dual challenges that have become the focal points for higher education in the initial decades of the 21st century. The simple fact is increasingly evident that the traditional face-to-face mode of the educational experience that many of us have seen as normative in higher education is long gone. We are in an era of leaning into a new norm, with a growing realization that equilibrium may be an increasingly fleeting commodity.

When we further narrow our discussion to the development of leaders for the Church, we must not look at quantitative information about learning effectiveness as a sole reference point. The context of the Church is people, and Scripture is quite clear about the Church being a community. Subsequently, some theological themes must be included in the discussion of what constitutes a viable and effective learning environment that will most likely yield influential leaders for the Church.

Genesis 1:27 provides us insight into humankind's distinctness in Creation. We are made in God's image. This signifies that humankind is made for relationships (with God and their fellow man) and ultimately responsible for that potential for relationships with the Creator and others. The impact of redemption is given visibility in communities that reflect God's purposes. From the Old Testament people of God to the New Testament church, these communities provide human visibility to God's redemptive plan, seen most clearly in Jesus Christ.

The research done by Dr. Day is the substance of this volume, which is strategically entitled *Remotely Close*. This volume looks at data that qualitatively evaluates learning occurring in online delivery formats and interfaces with the larger question of whether online learning alone effectively develops leaders for the Church of the 21st century. Dr. Day uses his own experiences of friendship that were the enduring benefit of his preparation for ministry. He is also well-experienced in learning through online delivery methods. He has a graduate and doctoral degree delivered exclusively through online means. The data on the current state of online learning describes the realities of developing leaders for the Church using online methodology. But there is a meta-question that hovers over the precise work, as it rightly should. How can current technology best enhance the development of leaders for the Church?

I commend Dr. Day's efforts to provide current data that interfaces with the larger theological questions that should be placed before anyone whose vocation is to develop Spirit-empowered leaders for the 21st-century Church.

PREFACE

Over the last 20+ years, I have served the local church, alongside my family, in pastoral ministry. Correspondingly, I have always wanted to learn and grow in every possible way by continuing my education. Not only do I enjoy learning, but it is a personal conviction that God has called all believers to be lifelong students of His Word and to remain hungry to become more knowledgeable in their various disciplines. After completing a bachelor's degree at a traditional on-campus university, my list of close personal friendships grew exponentially. Indeed, nothing in my life has impacted my growth in Christ, like the time I spent on that college campus for four years among such incredible women and men of God. Not only did I benefit in the short term from those connections, but many of them have remained as coaches, counselors, and mentors that I have leaned upon in my darkest days of ministry. On a practical note, every place of employment I have had the privilege of serving has materialized in one way or another as a direct result of the same group of friends. Therefore, the short-term and long-term benefits of my time at Bible College are immeasurable. As a mentor of mine once told me, "Life is all about relationships."

That said, not all of us are at a stage in life where we can uproot our families, quit our jobs, and enroll as full-time students on a traditional campus. Though many would love that opportunity, countless potential obstructions are standing between them and such a move. Time constraints, relational challenges, and often traditional educational approaches are far too expensive to consider. As a husband, father of two, and a full-time pastor, all the above factors were certainly on my radar. At the same time, the yearning and Divine calling to advance my education never waned. Therefore, as many of you will do, I continued my education and earned a Master's Degree and a Ph.D. through online means. I have ten years of online education (to date) at two universities. While I have benefited immensely from this season, there is a glaring distinction between my online and in-person experience. The difference? After ten years of online education that required no in-person cohorts, I could not point to one meaningful long-term friendship formed due to my time at two universities. This disappointed me greatly, presenting problems on at least three levels: personally, professionally, and theologically.

Firstly, I have come to know and experience the value of having friends. If I'm being honest, I would likely be selling used cars or life insurance right now if it were not for the support and encouragement of friends. (There is nothing wrong with selling cars or insurance; it is just not what God has called me to do.) The fact of the matter is, I would have quit the ministry a long time ago if it were not for my friends. One of our most challenging and confusing seasons of ministry was during the aftermath of the Global Pandemic of 2020. There was no handbook, class, conference, or seminar to prepare us to pastor a local church during a worldwide cataclysmic event. The thought of leaving my post crossed my mind on more than one occasion. The temptation to throw up my hands and declare, "This isn't worth it," was an ever-present possibility. What kept me steady and grounded in my calling were friends and mentors. God used these pivotal relationships to establish my calling and keep me strong when, in truth, I was very emotionally and spiritually burned out. There are not enough words in the English language, nor enough paper to write them upon, that would adequately express my gratitude to God for the gift of friendship.

Secondly, the absence of friendships gained through my online educational experience has affected me professionally. While gaining two more degrees may potentially open new doors of opportunity in the future, on a practical level, relationships are still essential as they relate to getting hired and growing a network of professional connections. The proceeding research offers evidence of this truth. While there is no doubt that information can be adequately attained through online/remote delivery systems, information alone does not always equate to real-world employment. The data shows that those in authority still hire primarily based on some relational connection, and very rarely do administrators hire their most important roles from a position of relational blindness, except in desperate situations.

Thirdly, and most importantly, the absence of friendships gained through my time as an online student bothers me on a theological level. Though I do not hold a terminal degree in theology (yet), fourteen of the seventeen contributors to this research project do possess earned doctorates in their various areas of Christian Leadership and/or Theology. Their keen insights into the matters of Biblical paradigms of ministry and leadership training are invaluable to this book, and it was my honor to interview and compile their collective wisdom on the subject. As I began to gather, process, and code many hours of one-on-one and group conversations, a clear and compelling pattern emerged. Not one contributor to this work argued for a Biblical precedent of learning in elongated seasons of isolation; instead, the opposite seems true. That is, learning within a community of like-minded believers appears to be the normative Biblical method of leadership development for God's Kingdom workers.

While it is true that God would lead prophets, priests, kings, and even His Son into seasons of solitude for spiritual purposes, the research laid before you in this book will articulate the differences between learning in isolation and being led by the Lord into temporary times of solitude to commune more closely with Him in prayer and fasting. It is clear and without dispute that the Apostle Paul and other leaders in Bible times wrote letters and taught via long-distance correspondence. No one is attempting to deny the credibility of this type of teaching method. That said, it would be very difficult to argue that the Biblical authors intended those writings to be read and processed in total isolation. Therefore, this book argues that

Christian Online Higher Education must be seasoned with relational elements to truly be in line with Biblical learning paradigms.

I am grateful that you are taking the time to read this book. I do not doubt that your shelves are filled with a long list of books that you'd likely enjoy much more than this one. So, let me begin by saying thank you for taking your precious time to read *Remotely Close*. I truly pray that this book is a blessing and a resource for readers as they embark on this learning journey and discover meaningful ways to connect with those with whom they learn in online classrooms. Furthermore, it is my great hope that once we (as Christian students and educators) discover the enduring benefits of adding purposeful relational elements to our online learning environments, we will never again return to anything less.

Dr. Daniel R. Day, Author
Ph.D. - Education & Organizational Leadership

INTRODUCTION

What do you suppose the following sayings or phrases have in common?

- Card Shark
- Irregardless
- First come, first serve
- Pawned off
- I could care less.
- The proof is in the pudding.
- That is not even remotely close.

Can you guess? They are all incorrect. Be honest, now. How many of you reading this page can admit to using these phrases in regular conversation? How many would be willing to fess up that you secretly judge people who use these incorrect sayings in your presence? Whether you are the offender of the English language or the offended grammar guru, the fact remains that these regularly misused sayings are incorrect either historically, grammatically, or both.

The correct version of card shark is card sharp, indicating that a person is skilled at playing cards. Irregardless is not a word at all. One should simply say, "regardless". First come, first serve should be first come, first served. The correct version of pawned off is palmed off, pointing to someone skilled at sleight of hand, a magician or trickster. If someone says they "could care less", they are actually saying they care. To be grammatically correct and in line with the meaning, one would need to say, "I couldn't care less". *The proof is in the pudding* is actually *the proof of the pudding is in the eating.* And finally, something cannot be remote and close simultaneously. The phrase, "That is not even remotely close," does not make sense...even remotely (see what I did there?). To be remote is to be far away and disconnected. Remotely close is an oxymoron, or is it?

Remote online education is undoubtedly here to stay. It is not going anywhere, and this book is not arguing that it should. There have always been those who need to access new training but are simply unable to be physically in an in-person classroom environment. Education through long-distance correspondence is not new, but as the technological delivery systems continue to advance and evolve rapidly, new challenges are presented, along with their consequent benefits. Educators must consider what crucial learning elements may have been lost in the rapid pursuit of convenient, accessible, and affordable remote/online education. Thus, the purpose of this book.

In no way does the research before you give evidence that in-person environments are better than online classrooms. The goal of this book is not to argue for a return to more traditional means of teaching. It is, however, seeking to highlight a vital element of the learning process that can be lost in typical remote/online education to the detriment of school administrators, learners, and professors. **Specifically, this work focuses on the relational component of education and its corresponding short-term and long-term benefits for all involved.** This research-based book shows that school administrators, teachers, and students have much to gain when strong relational connections exist. Therefore, based on the findings of my doctoral study, strategies are put forward to regain what remote education often is missing: relational closeness. I hope that this book may assist all involved in online education to become *remotely close.*

Before going any further, it would be helpful to define a few terms and outline the direction of this book. First, what is a *Remotely Close* Classroom? According to the study's findings, a remotely close online classroom is marked by an engaging and purposeful environment that assists students in the highest levels of academic achievement within the context of mutually beneficial relationships. To accomplish such a learning environment, policymakers and practitioners must first answer the pivotal questions of why, who, what, and how.

> A *remotely close* online classroom is marked by an engaging
> and purposeful environment that assists students in
> the highest levels of academic achievement within
> the context of mutually beneficial relationships.

Question 1: Why are relationships crucial to the online learning experience?

For those who participate in online higher education, be they leaders or learners, it is wise to begin by answering the question of *why*. In the following pages, a clear articulation of the benefits of relational closeness will be offered. The research will show that a remotely close classroom can only be achieved when administrators, online classroom designers, professors, and their students understand *why* it is imperative and worth their efforts to add relational components into their pedagogy. The short-term and long-term payoff equally applies to all; not one group only, but all.

Question 2: Who is responsible for creating the relational online classroom environment?

Each party must comprehend their unique roles and responsibilities related to cultivating an online classroom culture conducive to building friendships. No single group bears the total weight of responsibility. Administrators, designers, professors, and students can short-circuit relational closeness if they forgo their part. As you will see, the research findings are clear and convincing. A *remotely close* classroom can materialize only when all groups uphold their end of the bargain.

Question 3: What role does communication play in creating a *remotely close* classroom?

The third piece to this puzzle pertains to communication, specifically, the importance of how one may expect communication to occur. The question of personal and professional boundaries and how each group's preconceived notions of timing must all be covered before class beginning. This particular component is the axis upon which all of the others rotate. One must clearly articulate the communication protocols within the class so that students can connect in healthy ways with each other and their professors. But there are other channels of communication that are just as important. There are unique points to be made concerning how administrators speak with their staff and professors, how professors interact with administrators and their staff, and how the overarching leadership of the school communicates to their stakeholders and alums. Additionally, essential points about conflict management protocols are discussed in this section at length. A remotely close classroom cannot fully function at its highest potential without clear pathways to resolve conflict.

Question 4: How do those involved in the online classroom connect relationally?

The fourth and final characteristic of a remotely close classroom surrounds the idea of opportunity. When and where do students connect? Think of it this way. If you attended college on a traditional in-person campus, when and where did you make friends? How did relational opportunities organically happen? What social events were placed on the calendar to create chances for like-minded individuals to gather around a common interest? Do you have a mental picture of the times and places you met with friends? Now consider how you might recreate an online equivalent to such times and places. Is that even possible? The answer is yes, and that is the subject of this exciting section.

There is one final thought that I'd like to share before we jump into the meat of the matter. The sub-title of this book designates this effort as a *Christian* handbook for online higher education. During one of the many interviews conducted for this study, a participant asked, "What sets Christian online higher education apart from the others, and how would we know Christian online higher education when we saw it?" That interaction immediately seared itself into my heart and mind. It was a question I could not shake nor would it go away. Therefore, throughout this book, you'll see theological underpinnings giving voice to the true motivation behind a *remotely close* classroom. That motivation is to design our online learning environments to align with Biblical paradigms and protocols for leadership training. Are there constant, non-negotiable truths laced throughout the Scripture that offer God's strategic plan for creating Kingdom workers? And if so, they must also be present in our online schooling for a *remotely close* classroom to function correctly.

Being *remotely close* does not have to be an oxymoron any longer. Let's get started.

CHAPTER ONE

FOUNDATIONAL RESEARCH & CONCEPTS

Buy truth, and do not sell it— wisdom,
instruction and understanding.

PROVERBS 23:23 (ESV)

I n the months preceding the American Declaration of Independence, more than 11,000 British soldiers and hundreds of His Majesty's Navy filled the highways, byways, and Harbors in and around Boston, MA. For all points and purposes, the city was under the total control of England. General Washington noted that the enemy's defenses in the city were "amazingly strong...and almost impregnable, nearly every avenue fortified." [1] As the commander of the newly formed Continental Army agonized about how to penetrate and dislodge the entrenched enemy, he found himself in the company of a most unlikely fellow, Henry Knox – a gregarious bookseller from Boston.

Knox was a big man standing over six feet tall and weighing over 250 lbs. The only thing that outsized this 25-year-old Bostonian was his larger-than-life personality, which arrested the attention of all who had the pleasure of meeting him. Was he the well-groomed son of a military officer or a high-placed British family? Was he educated in the finest institutions of the land? Not at all – not even close. He was the seventh of ten sons to a shipmaster named William. When Henry's

1

father died, he was forced to leave school and go to work to support his struggling family. Henry became the apprentice to a bookbinder, and with this newfound employment, his journey of self-education began. [2] With nearly limitless access to books of all kinds, Knox became a consumer of all things military.

Knox joined a local militia following the battles of Bunker Hill and Concord. However, due to a hunting accident that severely injured his hand, Knox was limited in his physical abilities to fight. However, nothing would keep Henry from availing himself of his vast knowledge of military art, strategy, gunnery, and tactics. His keen and creative mind hatched a nearly impossible plan that gave General Washington the answer to his question regarding what to do about the city of Boston's unwelcomed and unyielding guests: the British military. At a meeting of the minds, General Washington invited his war council to convene and brainstorm ways to cause the enemy to depart Boston. Somehow, by some act of Providence, the young boisterous bookseller found himself in the room with the top leaders of the army.

As the meeting continued with little progress, a previously unknown voice billowed to the forefront. This untested and untried military novice spoke up with a creative idea. His proposition? Steal all the working guns from an abandoned fort on Lake Champlain, transport them 300-plus miles over lakes, rivers, mountains, and through marshes in the middle of a New England winter, and deliver them to Boston's Dorchester Heights. The administrative prowess needed to undertake such an enterprise is staggering, but even more unbelievable is the response of Washington to the ambitious and young Knox – "Yes". That November, Henry Knox, a self-educated bookseller with no previous military experience, was put in charge of one of the most critical top-secret missions that would turn the tide of the war. Many weeks later, Knox's "noble train" of 58 cannon weighing more than 120,000 lbs. arrived and was safely carried to General Washington. With these weapons, the General had what he needed. [3] Because of the omega efforts of Knox and his team, the British retreated from the city of Boston on March 17, 1776. Knox was continually promoted from that point on until the end of his career, becoming artillery commander, Major General, and the first-ever Secretary of War under President Washington. [4] When one hears a genuinely fantastic and inspirational account like this one, it gives rise to the self-made, pull-yourself-up-by-your-bootstrap beliefs about success and how it is attained. Knox appears to be a self-educated person who, through his own will and persistence, became mentally adept and savvy enough to climb to the very top of the civic and social ladder. For all practical purposes, Knox appears to be a positive example of a remote learner, absent of a learning community within a formal school. Or was he?

Years before the siege of Boston, Knox continued to grow and mature beyond the humble beginnings of his apprenticeship. This young and vivacious entrepreneur began one of Boston's most celebrated and frequented bookshops called *The London Bookstore*. [5] Not only did Knox entertain the daily presence of the British military, English Loyalists, and the social elite, but in this bookstore, he met his future wife, Abigail, and became friends with other well-known Bostonian leaders, such as Sam and John Adams.

Every day, all day, Knox was continually in an environment of conversation, rubbing shoulders with and processing the information he had been studying by engaging a political, social, and military cohort. While it is true that he had the intrinsic motivation to soak up all of the information he could through his reading and collecting of books, he purposefully built a social environment around himself to process his findings with those who lived out real-world applications of his knowledge. Somewhere along the way, this learning community became transformational and afforded Knox the confidence to advise the leading American generals of his generation. Furthermore, his advice led the way to one of the most treasured victories of the Revolutionary War.

Embedded within North American culture, the idea of a self-made overnight success story is celebrated and romanticized to the point that many have come to believe its validity. However, it is an idea that the research does not appear to support. Can a person be physically alone and learn simultaneously? Yes. However, the data suggests that adding the relational component to the educational process brings exponential benefits to all involved. In what follows, foundational research on online learning communities and the benefits of social integration are put forward.

THE RESEARCH PROBLEM

During one of the many interviews conducted for this study, a participant reminisced about the "old days" of long-distance education. This incredibly knowledgeable and skilled person who earned a doctorate and served his university for years in multiple roles as a dean, administrator, and teacher sat back in his chair and began to chuckle as he remembered the archaic remote learning methods he experienced. Years ago, he was earning a Master's degree through the distance learning modes of the day. Namely, everything was done through the mail...everything. The textbooks, curriculum, quizzes, tests, and written assignments were slowly and methodically worked through and mailed back to the university. Then he would have to wait (sometimes weeks) to get a reply, and only then would he find out the results of his assignments. This same pattern was repeated until finally, after years of work, this participant earned a Master's degree without any in-person interaction, not with fellow students or professors. It was all accomplished through the mail. Then, as he told me the story, he paused, leaned in, and said, "Even the lectures I watched were sent to me on VHS tapes that I watched on something called a VCR." (Should you be reading this and do not know what that means, please allow me to give you a word of advice...be kind and rewind. Still lost? Ask anyone 45 years old or older to explain.)

As the interview continued, he stated clearly that it was only after many years of reflection that he began to feel like he had missed out on an essential element of the learning process. At the time, he felt he was experiencing something innovative, convenient, and cost-effective. In some ways, he was doing just that. He genuinely felt happy when he graduated, having earned a higher educational degree without being forced to uproot his life. That said, as he told me the story further, he believes now that his entire learning experience and the long-term benefits of his MA would have been far greater if he could have benefited from a learning community with which to process the class information. In one sense, he feels robbed, having accomplished a degree in total social isolation.

Therein lies the problem, socially isolated learning and its potential mental, emotional, and educational impacts upon all involved. The research is convincing. Schools experience higher drop-out rates when students are negatively affected by socially isolated learning. [6] Professors articulated feelings of professional frustration and even abandonment, having been left to figure things out as they go and not being appropriately equipped by administrators to do their jobs. [7] For the online college student, social isolation has manifested in higher levels of loneliness, fear, anxiety, panic attacks, and even depression. [8] These are problems that stem from the same fundamental issue, human beings are inherently social creatures who desire to enjoy close and meaningful interaction and deep connection with one another. [9] (There is a strong Theological point to be made here, but more on that later.) When that intrinsic need is not fulfilled, and opportunities to process and learn in a community are removed, there are often negative and long-lasting consequences. [10] With online classes becoming more and more the rule rather than the exception, schools must make purposeful efforts to improve the overall feel of relational connectedness among their constituents. If the issues of social isolation caused by remote learning remain unaddressed, teachers and students may continue to suffer harm, and the school's mission may be misplaced and unattainable.

THE RESEARCH PURPOSE

The primary purpose of this research is to take a deep dive into the lived experiences, both good and bad, of those involved in Christian online university education. My goal is to see how learning remotely and wholly isolated from the broader educational community may impact 1) the academic performance of the student, 2) the professional satisfaction of the professor, and 3) the achievement of the school's overarching goals. Before we go further, allow me to take a moment to define a few key terms that will be used throughout the book. Then, I will outline the corresponding issues related to online education. Finally, this chapter will conclude by emphasizing the Christian priority of learning within a transformative community and how that Biblical paradigm applies to modern online educational goals.

Generally speaking, *social isolation* can be defined as a person's emotional and physical condition whereby they have chosen or been forced to withdraw themselves from all things familiar, like friends and family, for an excessive amount of time. [11] The findings of the study show that some will choose to gain their education through online remote learning due to their personal preference. In other words, due to their introverted social tendencies, learning remotely is very appealing. One of the participants in the study was just such a case; however, once she began her online journey, she discovered that she felt she was missing out on something fundamentally significant; namely, the benefit of the opinions and wisdom of fellow classmates. Others may enter online educational pathways due to their stage of life. Like me, they have a family, work a full-time job, and have other pressing commitments that prevent them from traditional on-campus means of education. Even though the convenience and accessibility of remote online learning are among some of the most important benefits of such delivery tools, that does not mean that the benefits of a learning community diminish or Biblical paradigms of education change based on someone's stage of life. Thus, the impetus for this research. Through this study, I have sought to find the balance between modern online learning delivery systems and normative Biblical designs for education. Furthermore, this book will argue that when this balance is achieved, there are multiple short-term and long-term benefits to be experienced by all involved.

Next, I would like to clarify and define a few terms that will be used for the remainder of the book so that the reader may have a reference point and better understand the study's framework. While this is not an exhaustive list of terms on online education, these became the most pertinent for the study at hand. Other scholars may vary in their opinions of the following list. They may add to or take away from the following definitions. That said, the summation of the terminology is rooted in multiple recent scholarly literature and provides a solid foundation moving forward.

LIST OF TERMS

Academic Engagement signifies that the student has a great sense of intrinsic self-motivation to interact with all points of their academic experiences and learning material. [12]

Academic performance refers to the student's ability to fully and systemically comprehend, understand, and apply what they have learned in their class context. [13]

Academic Persistence/Resilience refers to the progression of and ability of the student's flexibility and adaptation despite complex challenges. [14] It may also indicate one's aptitude for successfully handling academic setbacks, anxiety, and pressures. [15] Furthermore, it is a student's ability to be blindsided and simultaneously cope and maintain their academic schedule and structure. [16]

Distance Education refers to officially endorsed and accredited education in which those in the class (learners and leaders) are not in the same physical learning environment. [17]

Extracurricular Activities are events outside the regular curriculum of a school or college: sports, music, clubs, and drama are examples of some of the most prevalent extracurricular activities. [18]

Faculty and Staff Relations: The faculty and staff of the online program are the principal players in fostering a safe, exciting, and interactive community within the classroom for the students. [19] Important relational factors include a sense of trust fostered by honest dialogue, empathy, grace, and a commitment to healthy conflict management. [20]

Online/eLearning/remote delivery tools are the systems that facilitate and strengthen learning with digital technologies. [21]

Intellectual development refers to the personal intellectual growth of the student beyond one's personal firmly held preexisting ignorance, prejudice, or biases as a result of their learning and interactions at school. [22]

Peer-group interactions mean having the opportunity to work together in collaborative environments inside the classroom with their fellow learners [23], as well as engaging with them outside the classroom through informal social gatherings. [24]

Remote learning refers to giving and receiving education through non-traditional means via technological delivery systems without an in-person/face-to-face classroom experience. [25]

Social integration refers to how a student develops into a fully accepted, respected, and valuable part of the class, group, and overall educational and social structure. [26] When the learner has attained a high level of acceptance and respect by involving themselves in the institutional social structure and feels a great sense of appreciation and care from their peers and professors, they can be considered socially integrated. [27]

Sense of Belonging refers to when the student feels accepted and connected to their peers and professors, as well as to the overall social ethos of the institution. One may be considered connected when they feel they are relating well with the school's community by having high trust and mutual support. [28]

Social isolation (SI) refers to a person's emotional and physical condition, whereby they have chosen or been forced to withdraw themselves from all things familiar, like friends and family, for excessive time. [29] SI records and refers to the absence of social interactions or uncommon social contact with other people, accentuated by an acute sense of loneliness. [30]

Student engagement is when the student gives their utmost focus, care, and thoughtfulness to the study materials being presented and involves the cumulative effort the learner puts into their overall achievement and success. [31]

Professor engagement: This type of interaction involves students' positive back-and-forth relationship with the teacher of the courses in which they are enrolled. [32]

Having laid the foundation and offered a reference point for key terms, I will outline the study participants and contributors. These amazing men and women made an indelible mark upon the research findings, and I am eternally grateful for them.

THE RESEARCH PARTICIPANTS

The data presented here results from a one-and-a-half-year doctoral research project. Following a thorough analysis of the existing body of scholarly literature on the connection between one's social isolation and academic success within online learning environments, seventeen purposefully selected participants were invited and agreed to contribute to the study's findings. Two primary sample groups emerged: A leader group and a learner group. Some participants met the qualifications for both sample groups. Therefore, their life experiences added value to both sets of data. A qualified leader group participant had at least one year of experience teaching post-secondary online education. Faculty, staff, and administrators were welcome to participate if they had at least one year of experience facilitating online education for their college. The learner group comprised men and women who had taken at least two online classes that required no in-person class time. Among those in the leader group, there was an average of 7.6 years of online teaching experience and 5.4 years of online classroom design and administration, and they had been employed at a minimum of 2.2 colleges/universities. The learner group had an average of 2.7 years of experience taking college classes online. Let the reader know that no names of the participants or the schools that they have worked with will be shared in this book. Their privacy is part of a signed agreement to protect their identities and thereby allow for open dialogue on the subject matter. Contributors to this study will be referred to as participant, interviewee, or contributor throughout the book. However, I've included a general synopsis of each participant's educational background in *Appendix 1* so that the reader may understand the depth of knowledge and experience that each one brought to the study.

THE RESEARCH PRIORITY

Please note that this book has a solidly Christian priority. As the author, I believe that learning within a community of mutually beneficial relationships both honors God and sharpens the group as iron sharpens iron. [33] It is my informed conviction that there is a Biblical precedence for this type of learning. Blessing is sure to follow when this principle is applied to modern educational tools. There may be outlier examples of individuals in the Scripture who were brought into lonely and secluded places for short seasons to commune more closely with the Lord through fasting and prayer. However, that is different from elongated times of isolated individual leadership training and preparation. If ever there was a person who walked the earth and could have accomplished everything on His own, it would be Jesus Christ. Nevertheless, even He chose to enter our world, live and learn within the context of His family[34] and local synagogues. [35] When His time for public ministry began, He set the tone and example by choosing to work with a team. [36] The idea of the lone ranger leader or learner is not the Biblical norm.

For clarity's sake, I am not arguing that learning alone through remote correspondence is sinful, wrong, or completely unhelpful. It is not my goal to bring unwarranted condemnation into anyone's life. I sincerely hope to articulate the extreme blessings and benefits that one gains by following Scriptural norms and applying them to modern educational pathways. Can someone learn information alone? Yes. Does that information potentially take the learner to new heights in their personal, spiritual, and professional development? The research suggests that this *is* the case. However, the findings also suggest that when one adds the Biblical paradigm of learning within a healthy social community, the potential benefits increase exponentially. Furthermore, if we ignore this principle, we may inadvertently short-circuit our growth and stifle future opportunities to be used in greater measure by the Lord. I pray that this book will strongly highlight the great blessings and benefits that come when one understands God's design for education within the context of community.

DISCUSS & JOURNAL

DISCUSSION

In your journal, respond to the definition of a *remotely close* classroom. How can you and your team work together to create a more engaging and purposeful online environment for your students?

<u>Definition</u>: A *remotely close* online classroom is marked by an engaging and purposeful environment that assists students in the highest levels of academic achievement within the context of mutually beneficial relationships.

JOURNAL

_____

_____

_____

_____

_____

_____

_____

_____

_____

_____

_____

_____

_____

CHAPTER TWO

THE BENEFITS OF AN ONLINE LEARNING COMMUNITY

How much better to get wisdom than gold! To get
understanding is to be chosen rather than silver.

PROVERBS 16:16 (ESV)

At some point in your education, you were likely taught about the battles of Lexington and Concord, the first official skirmishes of the American Revolution that an unknown soldier started with the "shot heard around the world." [1] I would like to take a moment and share a lesser-known story that took place a little over a year after this historical turning point. I call it the shot not heard around the world. In 1776, muzzle-loading smooth-bore firelock muskets were carried by the rank-and-file military of the day. However, Major Patrick Ferguson of the British Army was no average soldier. His custom-made breach-loading rifle with its seven-grooved bore that could spin a ball with pinpoint accuracy was no ordinary weapon. Major Ferguson was the most accomplished English marksman of the time, and with his excellent eye and personalized weapon of choice, he could hit a piece of paper 200 yards away four times a minute. When Ferguson put something in his sights, he did not miss. This 18th-century sniper was a living lethal weapon.

One brisk morning, on September 11, 1777, Major Ferguson was on a reconnaissance mission to scout out the US Rebel position along the Brandywine Creek Valley just south of Philadelphia. From his hidden position, he spotted two easy targets riding towards him only 100 yards away—an easy shot for Ferguson. Judging by their dress, the two unsuspecting men were Continental Army officers riding towards the most decorated British marksman of a generation.

As the Major readied his weapon, Ferguson, ever the gentleman soldier, cried out a warning to the riders. Should they continue, they would meet a swift end. The US senior officer remained composed and calm. The mounted US Rebel continued coolly about his business without wavering or withdrawing. Presenting Fergusson with no sporting challenge, no fleeting or retreating target to fire upon, this stately British officer felt it would be wrong to kill him. Though he could have fired half a dozen rounds into his enemy before he could escape to safety, Fergusson allowed his enemy to carry on. He chose not to take his shot and allowed the riders to live.

The British sniper was on a lone reconnaissance mission. You might say that he was an isolated learner, gaining intel to make better-informed future decisions for his company. Was he able to learn some things on his own? Yes. He was able to learn the whereabouts of the Continentals, as well as a few other essential details. On some levels, his mission was a success. This lone learner returned to his camp and reported back to the group. Later that same day, Fergusson learned that the man he held in his sights that morning was General George Washington and his aide-de-camp. Had the British Major known, his gentlemanly code of honor may have been neglected. [2] I am not saying that Fergusson did not or could not learn important bits of information while he was alone. Rather, he could learn *more* when he processed the same information with a group of peers. If he had that extra piece of info when General Washington was in his sights, the entire course of history would likely be very different.

Imagine how the outcome of our lives may have been different if Fergusson had made another choice. Simply stop for a moment and consider that question. Washington had no idea he was in the sights of the deadliest and most accurate sharp-shooter in the world's most powerful army. But by some act of God's Providence, his life was spared. I, for one, am eternally grateful for that fact. Perhaps Major Fergusson did not miss many targets during his illustrious and storied career, but he did miss this opportunity to change the course of history.

The goal of Chapter 2 is to highlight the numerous benefits and rewards of learning and processing information within a community of mutually beneficial relationships, as opposed to social isolation. I hope that once the reader sees and understands the enormous short-term and long-term rewards that emerge from a learning community like this, the reader will not miss out on the opportunity to change the course of their own journey for the better. Various benefits for online professors, students, and administrators were noted throughout the study's numerous journal entries, one-on-one interviews, and group chats. All seventeen contributors to this research believed that their online educational experience was greatly enhanced or hindered due to having formed or not formed relationships with peers and professors. What follows is an outline of their contribution to the study's findings and how these findings correspond with recent scholarly literature.

Five primary common themes were generated from the participants' talking points, which included 1) finding and keeping employment, 2) future networking opportunities, 3) social and spiritual support systems, 4) lower attrition/higher graduation rates, and 5) higher professional satisfaction. As the data collection process unfolded, it became abundantly clear that there was significant personal, professional, and spiritual value to having strong relational connections throughout the online educational experience. The data gathered from the contributors to the doctoral study was in sync with previous research, with the addition of a uniquely Christian perspective. Though mentioned several times by four of the participants that people with introverted personalities or incredibly complex schedules may not have the time nor the desire to build new relationships within their online classes, all 17 contributors to the study agreed that the educational experience that comes from availing one's self of relationships is more beneficial in the long run.

FINDING AND KEEPING EMPLOYMENT

This particular category of Finding and Keeping Employment was one of the leading motivating factors as it related to choosing the research topic. A nagging question continued to bubble up in my mind. Do people attain a higher employability factor due to learning in a community instead of learning in social isolation? While, at the beginning of my research, I did not have any hard data to prove it, my gut told me that there was a direct correlation between one's relationships and one's employability. That has certainly been my personal experience throughout my career as a minister and educator, but I did not have the evidence yet to prove it. Now I do, and the irrefutable data underscores that one gains more professional opportunities in life when they have a sizeable relational network.

When asked about this subject, one participant noted, "If you lack a network of peers, that can be detrimental to you being hired in the field. Once you are done with your program, your peers often become colleagues in whatever you are doing. When students do not have those friendships or some level of connection with their peers, it could put them at a disadvantage if they do not have those working networks before graduation." Two other interviewees agreed and took ample time to explain that students have an easier time finding employment upon graduation when strong bonds of relationships have been formed during their time at college. These findings agree with previous scholarship that learners greatly benefit from the active formation of new friendships and professional contacts by participating in the overall ethos of the classroom and broader school culture. [3] The data shows that students have more professional opportunities upon the completion of their schooling when relationships are strong, but the benefits do not stop there. At the risk of sounding like an infomercial...but wait... there is more!

Not only do relationships help one find a job upon graduation, but the study also revealed another critical data point. Relational bonds assist one in keeping a job once it is found. As one former dean of a major university stated, he was acutely aware of the importance of professor-to-student relationships and the ramifications those relationships had for the professor's employment. He stated, "Many schools will base the hiring of online professors upon student course evaluations. Moreover, if you are an online adjunct, there is a good chance you are not creating content, and you are not just there to give grades but to help students learn. You get a teaching contract the next semester because you received a 4.9 and not a 4.1 on your course evaluation scores. The benefit is simple: you keep your job." He pointed out that universities do not have any shortage of highly qualified applicants for adjunct online positions. Therefore, contracts to teach are usually on a semester-by-semester basis. If the online professor does not go above and beyond to connect with each student, it will likely affect their course evaluation scores and future employability. He said the online professor "lives and dies" by this ever-present factor. Thus, gaining and keeping one's employment is directly impacted by relational connections. That leads one to ask how online learning communities add value to this point? That is the subject of the next section.

FUTURE NETWORKING OPPORTUNITIES

The second sub-theme for this category pointed to the benefit of professional networking within online learning environments. As I previously mentioned, over the last 20+ years, all of the jobs I have had the privilege of performing have come about as a direct or indirect result of the friendships/networks created during my time at Bible College. Those relationships meant the difference between employment and unemployment. At the outset of my study, I wondered if others had experienced a similar journey. As conversations began to take place, it became abundantly clear that most could agree with or personally relate to my own story. Three interviewees drew attention specifically to the advantage of friendships gained during the online educational experience. One stated, "The networking capacity has long-term value." Another agreed, saying, "Networking and relationships are ultimately quite important to getting anywhere within a vocation. I think that relationships are important for anyone going through an educational journey, especially in an online program, because beyond your degree program, your network and those relationships that you have built with peers and professors will hopefully continue to serve you beyond that." Another participant recalled, "For those that might be looking for new employment opportunities, they interact with other students in their field. There are networking opportunities; another benefit is receiving their personal recommendation." But what further value might there be to these networks of friends gained during college beyond getting hired at a good company? It is a great question, because it is not enough to get a good job. To remain professionally motivated and relevant, one needs a support system. Therein, one discovers the next great benefit to learning in a social community.

SOCIAL AND SPIRITUAL SUPPORT SYSTEMS

In the aftermath of the Global Pandemic of 2020, many of my friends in the ministry began to show signs of tremendous discouragement. Some went as far as resigning their positions out of incredible frustration and professional disillusionment. That said, it was not just pastors who felt this way; anyone whose life was disrupted by unknown factors related to the COVID-19 disease appeared to be in the same rocky boat. What ensued became known as the *Great Resignation*. [4]

According to the United States Bureau of Labor Statistics, 47 million Americans voluntarily exited the workforce in 2020/21, resulting from the Pandemic. [5] Nearly every major category of employment was affected, and that included the church at large. One study by the Barna Research group showed that 42% of pastors seriously considered quitting during the great resignation. [6] One by one, many of my friends in the ministerium grew disheartened by growing calls from various factions of the church to wear masks, or do not wear masks, isolate, or do not isolate, shake hands, or do not shake hands, social distance, or do not social distance, vaccinate, or do not vaccinate, and so on and so on and so on. The never-ending feeling of failing or disappointing people they loved dearly was constantly on their minds. Most pastors I know did not go into the ministry to make people mad, but there was a time when many of my friends felt like that was all they could do during the Pandemic. It did not matter what type of leadership choices they made; someone in the congregation was going to get offended, someone was going to complain, someone was going to get angry. Someone would leave the church and find a *real* man of faith. This type of situation can exact a high emotional toll, and some of my minister friends decided they had had enough. If you knew half the stories I do about how some congregations treated their pastors during this time, you would not blame them for quitting. I, for one, do not stand in judgment against them. Some congregations were very cruel to their shepherds. After much self-inspection, I must admit that looking into other forms of employment crossed my mind more than once. What kept me steady and secure in my calling and vocation came down to the subject of this section: social and spiritual support structures.

Not only does the research show that learning within a social community helps graduates to find and keep employment and build professional networks, but these networks go on to provide the basis for the next category, social and spiritual support systems. [7] Ten of the 17 participants in the study took time to emphasize the tremendous role that social and spiritual support systems played in their online education and beyond. One participant said, "I really think it is vital to the student success, not just academically, but spiritually, emotionally, mentally, just staying in a healthy place." When one participant recalled a moment when they seriously wanted to quit their online educational journey, they said what kept them going was the realization that "I am not alone. Other people on this journey are experiencing the same thing. It is hard, but I can get through this now because I am journeying with others." Again, another interviewee stated, "There were days I was going to quit, and then we would just cheer each other on. So, as far as completing the schooling, we also had each other's support." One professor highlighted that students, "need that social interaction and accountability. Often, students will want to connect with other students because they are going through the same thing, they feel the same pain, and there is a lot of empathy, interaction, and encouragement for one another." Others discussed how these same support groups that kept them from quitting their education have continued well beyond graduation and into their prospective careers. Some still regularly pray with each other and call upon those friendships in times of great difficulty and stress. This has certainly been my personal experience as well. If it were not for the social and spiritual support structures formed during Bible School, I would likely not be in the ministry today.

LOWER ATTRITION/HIGHER GRADUATION RATES

All of the college administrators interviewed in this research project concur with those studied in previous scholarly articles that enrollment of new students and the retention of current students are two subjects that are constantly on the minds of those at the top of the leadership ladder. [8] The findings of the research agree, as students who have solid relationships with classmates and professors are far more likely to graduate than those who learn in complete isolation. [9] Furthermore, not only do the socially connected have a higher graduation rate, but they finish in a higher state of emotional, mental, and spiritual wellness. [10] One interviewee highlighted this point when she said that the friendships she had formed in the online program were "the most important factor for successfully finishing on time and doing so in a healthy way." This same participant went on to articulate concerns; she had seen classmates graduate with very little emotional capital left in the tank. While they might have crossed the finish line by earning a degree, they appeared to be so burned out by the end that applying that newly found knowledge/skill in the real world would be difficult. [11] The difference? Relational learning communities. [12] Three other contributors drew connections between relationships and completing an online program. One stated that they had seen "the percentage of students staying in the course, pressing through and finishing increases" for those in a learning community. Another emphasized what he called the "longevity factor" and believed that when strong relationships exist, there is not only an increase in graduation rates but one's longevity in one's prospective occupation after graduation. In other words, they graduate with the passion and the fire in their hearts to go out into the world and do what the Lord has called them to do. They finish well and with emotional health. [13]

HIGHER PROFESSIONAL SATISFACTION

For this final section of the chapter, I will begin by posing a question to those of you who are current educators or plan to become vocational teachers. Why? Can you answer the question of why you want to become a teacher? Was your answer money? If so, you might want to reevaluate that response. According to one recent study, more than a 3rd of online professors live below the poverty line, while 40% of online adjuncts struggle to afford average household needs. [14] Was your answer fame? Again, high levels of notoriety and celebrity are not likely in the life of an educator. There is nothing wrong with having hopes of one day making a significant contribution to scholarly works, but the data indicates that successful teachers need to have something internally driving their desire to teach. So, what motivates you to enter a vocation that will not likely make you rich or famous? My research affirmed what we all likely know intrinsically, and that is people typically become teachers out of a sense of calling and desire to make a difference in the lives of the next generation. [15] That said, when a system of online education reduces the professor to someone who reads and grades assignments, that system has the potential to emotionally gut the professor of that which motivates them in the first place. Professional satisfaction climbs, and teachers are far more willing to perform above and beyond the call of duty when they see that their students are connecting on a relational level that brings about life-on-life transformation. [16]

The fifth category, under academic and relational benefits, highlights the connection between professional satisfaction and the online learning community. Four interviewees explained that their feelings of professional satisfaction were much higher when relational connections were strong. One adjunct professor said, "I agree that for your average professor who does want to connect with people, and particularly in a Christian educational environment, I am sure the reason the professor is doing it is because he or she wants to have some kind of life-on-life influence beyond just what they have written and how they respond on assignments." He went on to further clarify that he longed, "to have a sense that [he was] influencing, encouraging, and lifting people." Moreover, this professor and others reiterated that the only way to get that sense [of life-on-life influence] is through feedback that comes through the relational cycle. Thus, teaching online without a close relational connection with their students is a deterrent for them even wanting to teach [online] in the first place because it just does not fit their personality.

Participants lamented that the overall negative relational elements of online teaching make the administrative parts of teaching online classes even more burdensome. The absence of relational closeness makes seeing the return on investment very difficult. Some interviewees would rather devote their time and efforts to educational systems that allow authentic connections between themselves and their students. In the life experience of another adjunct professor, the belief is, "If I am called to be a teacher, then I get my fulfillment from doing what I am called to do. Thus, the goal is not the information we are unpacking but the person we are bringing to maturity. Now, yes, we are using knowledge to impart to them to bring it to maturity, but it is still about the person, not about the knowledge. So, if we as teachers do not have that as our driving motivation, we are in the wrong place." One online college administrator underscored this idea further, saying, "Most of the people I have engaged with and worked with as instructors got into online teaching because they had some desire to pass on knowledge and experience to the next generation of ministry leaders." This philosophy was reinforced by the experiences of yet another interviewee when they said, "I think anyone in the teaching vocations can see a difference between a job and a calling. A job means that I'm just going to check the boxes, give them minimum input, and get through the course so I get paid. However, if it is a real calling and you want to develop your students, it is important to stay connected with them as much as possible." Finally, another contributor to the study remarked, "I just think the more you engage, the more you will reap. Moreover, I believe with all my heart that it [relationships] is a vital part of online education."

Finding and keeping employment, future networking opportunities, social and spiritual support systems, lower attrition/higher graduation rates, and higher professional satisfaction are beneficial. These five primary benefits of learning within an online educational community represent the common thread that weaves through previous scholarly literature and my doctoral study. Can a student learn information in isolation? Yes. Does that information learned have the potential to impact the isolated learner positively? Sure. This research offers evidence that the student experiences a better educational journey, teachers have a higher level of professional satisfaction, and schools are far more likely to achieve their organizational goals when a healthy relational online learning community is everyone's mutual priority. All three of these groups (administrators, professors, and students) have an opportunity to alter the trajectory of their collective futures for the better. As we will see in the next chapter, we all have a part to play and responsibilities to perform. Now that you have looked at some of the tremendous long and short-term benefits of learning in a healthy online community, I hope you will have adequate inspiration to take your shot and not miss your moment to change the course of history.

DISCUSS & JOURNAL

DISCUSSION

With which of the five primary benefits can you most relate? *Brainstorm with your team*. Can you think of other benefits that have not been listed?

<u>The Five Benefits</u>: 1) finding and keeping employment, 2) future networking opportunities, 3) social and spiritual support systems, 4) lower attrition/higher graduation rates, and 5) higher professional satisfaction.

JOURNAL

_____

_____

_____

_____

_____

_____

_____

_____

_____

_____

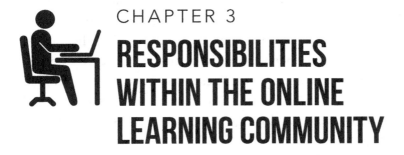

CHAPTER 3

RESPONSIBILITIES WITHIN THE ONLINE LEARNING COMMUNITY

For each will have to bear his own load.

GALATIANS 6:5 (ESV)

Many remarkable stories have come from the famed 1936 Olympics hosted by Nazi Germany. People like runner Jesse Owens, who not only won four gold medals but did it as a black man under the long shadow of Hitler's 3rd Reich, who believed that Owens was somehow inferior to their "superior" race. Jesse was a fierce and focused competitor that went on to set 4 new world records. He also set another record straight in the process: Jesse was inferior to no one. [1] Thirteen-year-old Marjorie Gestring of the U.S. team won the gold medal in springboard diving and still holds the record for youngest female gold medalist in the history of the Summer Olympic Games. [2] Louis Zamperini's moving story was brought to the silver screen in 2014 in the movie *Unbroken*. While he never medaled in the games, his acts of valor in the U.S. armed forces earned him several medals for his gallant service in WWII. [3] In all, the U.S.A. took home 56 total medals (24 Gold) in 1936 [4], but out of all these inspirational true stories, one stands out in my mind as it applies well to our next topic: *responsibility*.

The 9-man rowing team from the University of Washington (U of W) stunned the world when they won gold. This unlikely moment is recorded in Daniel Brown's book entitled, *The Boys in the Boat*, which recounts the story of how 9 American boys who originated from poor, hardworking families of logging camps, sawmills, and shipyards rose to win what was at the time, the most coveted medal of the games. Some of these boys had been living on their own since they were abandoned in their childhood years. These were not the well-groomed children of White-collar America. They were sons of struggle and hardship, clawing their way through the Great Depression. Whatever they had, they earned by the sweat of their brow and a tenacity for survival. Before coming to college, none of these boys had ever been on a rowing team, and yet, when they found each other in the boat house as freshmen at U of W, something special transpired. These boys, who had been forged in the fires of adversity, channeled their collective strength into the oars of the boat. What happened next stunned the nations.

The 9-man rowing team defeated the 2-time champs, the University of California. They went on to defeat the Ivy League Schools in the North East, crushing records as they went. Even the best schools in England (Oxford and Cambridge) could not keep up. After going through a gauntlet of competition, they finally won the right to represent the U.S.A. in Germany. In one of the most stunning comeback stories of all time, these unlikely American heroes etched their names into the pages of sports history and brought home the honor of gold. How was it possible for such a fantastic story to have taken place? As one of their coaches remarked,

> Everything came together. The right oarsmen, with the right attitudes, the right personalities, the right skills. They had the perfect boat, sleek, balanced, and wickedly fast. A winning strategy and coxswain with the guts and smarts to

make hard decisions and make them fast. It all added up to
something far beyond the sum of its parts. [5]

Alone, each crew member was incredibly strong and fast on the water, but together, they were *stronger* and *faster* than anyone in the world. Were they skilled rowers on their own? Yes. As a matter of fact, all nine were tremendously fast as individual rowers. Simply put, they were *better* together. It was said by those who watched this legendary crew that their boat seemed to be a living, breathing creature on the water as they rowed, as though they had become one with the boat, and it was about to lift right out of the water and take flight.

That said, there was a danger, a hidden "Achilles' heel," in this particular sport. Namely, focus. If even *one* team member did not fully concentrate on the task at hand, everything would fall apart. It only took one person having a bad day to bring the entire boat to a halt.

One of the fundamental challenges in rowing is that when
any one member of the crew goes into a slump, the entire crew
goes with him. Each of the rowers has a slightly different role,
depending on his position in the boat, and each of these roles
is critical. One wrong move from any one person can disrupt
the course, speed, and stability of the boat. [6]

Who was responsible for bringing the boat across the finish line? All of them. How many people did it take to bring it all to a halt... only *one*. It only took one person who did not hold up their end of the responsibility to turn what could be great into something mediocre.

Now that we've covered why learning within an online community benefits all involved, we will now consider the question of *who*. When it comes to creating a relationally oriented online classroom community, who is responsible for its success or failure? Let's dive in.

RELATIONAL & ACADEMIC RESPONSIBILITY

In this section, the research will provide answers to the question of responsibility, specifically, who is responsible for bringing people together relationally in online educational environments. The study revealed that this burden does not rest on one person or group. According to the findings, online students and professors have the best chance of being socially engaged when the following three entities *cooperate* to bring people together. Like the boys rowing in a boat, the entire effort collapses if even one loses focus. The three primary groups that carry the shared responsibility for building the remotely close classroom include school administrators, professors, and students. While the research suggests that no one person shoulders the entire load, it only takes one group not doing their part to significantly hinder the relational potential that might be there if they were to fulfill their role.

ADMINISTRATIVE RESPONSIBILITY

Nine of the 17 contributors to the study highlighted the importance of school administration and their role in equipping professors with the tools needed to facilitate quality online education and relational experiences. In building relationships with others in the online class, one participant said this issue is "probably the biggest hurdle to online education in my experience." The findings reveal the need for administrators to look at the bigger picture of online education, reevaluate it, and consider it in a new light. According to another contributor, "I am concerned. I am honestly concerned about the big picture that the rush to accessibility and affordability has decreased the authentic holistic value of an education. Moreover, it is unfortunately created or lent to the creation of a very transactional approach to learning. Online learning is so susceptible to transactional learning." According to my research, there are four areas that administrators must reconsider should they desire to see the benefits of a remotely close classroom at work in their school. 1) Technology, 2) In-class assistance, 3) Peer mentors, and 4) Flexibility.

Issue 1: Technology. Throughout the interview process, an apparent disconnect existed between those who created the online Learning Management System (L.M.S.) and classroom design and those who did the actual teaching. One interviewee said, "I want to put this delicately. I do not know if I have ever met a senior administrator who has created or taught an online class. It really bugs me. We lose all of our best teachers to administration because that is how you get noticed and promoted, and we end up decapitating the academic house. Five to ten years down the line, we have an administration that has not been in a classroom for five to ten years." Another contributor lamented, "I spend more time navigating the L.M.S. than teaching. And that is the most significant frustration of teaching online. Learning management systems have all kinds of bells and whistles created by technology wizards that are all cute and exciting. However, when it comes to using those in a learning system, they have been created by technology experts rather than educational experts. So, my intrinsic motivation is not there when I spend half my time navigating an L.M.S. I will find ways to continue my work without the burden of all that technological side." Past research, as well as my own, shows that many online professors do not sense that they have been adequately trained to manage the technology intended to be the tool to help them do their job. [7] This point reveals that it is the first and primary responsibility of the administration to equip and train their professors to the point that they feel confidently able to maximize the technological tools for teaching purposes.

Issue 2: In-Class Assistance. Secondly, there was an overall sense among online professors that they could not give their students the full benefit of their wisdom and experience due to the time needed to read and grade assignments. During one interview, this professor relayed an excellent experience: "The optimal arrangement is a professor and a teaching assistant. The teaching assistant can do a lot of the grading, or in my case, I had a wonderful assistant. She would pre-grade things for me going through and kind of get a general feel of where the work was, and then I would be responsible for the primary grade. Then, I focused on student feedback." Therefore, because this professor was not overly burdened with the initial grading, creative ideas like individual video/ podcast feedback from the professor to each student could transpire. This allowed for more one-on-one and undivided attention to be given to all in the class, which inevitably led to closer relationships.

Issue 3: Peer Mentors. Thirdly, the findings revealed that online professors felt the most isolated, not from their students but from their school's administrative leadership. During one interview, an online professor stated, "One of the challenges of institutions that utilize online instruction is how we come together and make people feel apart and sense the value of the different people with whom we interact." Additionally, another interviewee bemoaned that while working at a prominent university, "It was awkward to ask for help. It did not seem like they [the administration] wanted to help me. That is where I did feel isolated. I understood that the culture of that [university] tended to be more standoffish, and they are not warm and welcoming." While working for a different university, another participant in the study shared this excellent experience. "It is nice in a community where you can provide feedback and have consistent periodic meetings. You have that opportunity to glean from others that have been farther down the road than you have in education." In this case, the professor enjoyed regular staff/faculty/administration meetings for mutual professional development. This was an example of a positive peer mentor experience. One former college president encouraged all those in administration, "Everything rises and falls on leadership...I have always been encouraged to create, to provide opportunities for peers to connect."

Issue 4: Flexibility. The data revealed an overwhelming consciousness of rigidity from those in higher educational administration about their approach to and philosophy of online education. Professors were made to feel that their superiors were only interested in continuing to do what has always been done when new ideas may improve online programs. One interviewee said, "I think it [online education] has to continue to innovate. I think it would become negative for me if we were no longer interested in innovating, and we just wanted to do what we have always been doing, and we were no longer offering a good product to our students." While it is true that no one entity can force relationships upon any participant in online education, the findings of this study reveal that it is the responsibility of educational administrators to equip professors with the necessary tools for the job. One participant suggested, "I would love to see a class in every program on doing this and instruction for professors on how to create the experiences virtually that would make it easier for relationships to develop." Again, one contributor stated, "The burden of this [making friends], the onus is on the student, but the opportunity is certainly being provided on [by L.M.S.] platforms." Therefore, if the tools for continued professional development, accountability, and relationships are given to the professors, the professors and their students will be more likely to form meaningful relationships in class.

That said, administrators are only holding one of the oars in the boat. There are two more groups to consider. The next major group that holds some of the responsibility to give everyone their best chance of developing long-term and meaningful friendships is professors.

PROFESSOR RESPONSIBILITY

Participants 1, 4, 6, 8, 9, 12, 13, 15, 16, and 17 underscored the significance of the online professor and the indelible part that they play in facilitating strong relational connections for themselves and their students that can lead to higher levels of learning for the student and professional satisfaction for the teacher. The central issue of motivation was strongly addressed by Participant 13 when they said that it is all about "investing in the next generation" and how a professor must have a personal "stake in the success of those who follow after you." If the online professor only performs the "minimum online requirements," they only provide a sub-par or "minimal online experience" for their students. The research findings revealed four primary practices that successful online professors employ in their classes to create meaningful interaction between themselves and their learners.

Self-Leadership Practice 1: A Personal Connection. For participants 4, 6, and 12, adding a unique personal connection could not be overemphasized. Offering multiple avenues by which the students can reach the professor can put students at ease, thereby removing one more layer of stress from the student experience. Participant 12 recalled, "One of the things that I have heard in my few years in online education leadership is that students dislike courses where it is hard to contact the professor, or it seems like the professor is absent from the course. It, for some students, causes a great deal of anxiety because they are wondering, okay, what grade do I have in this class?" The remedy for such worry was easy for Participant 6. It meant they made extra space in their schedule for the students to ask questions and process material. Participant 6 says, "I do feel like when I extended myself with more access, and people would take advantage of that, that did help to give a sense of different kinds of relationships again." When this type of access and communicative rapport exists between students and professors, the connection takes on a new importance. Participant 4 noted that students "are hungering for a mentor ." The closer the student relates to the professor, the more Participant 4 believed that the class could become a "transformational" experience for the student. As Participant 11 recalled multiple educational moments at more than one college as a student, "when I think back, I don't think about who the administrator was. I think about who my professor was, and that's my identity with the school itself. So, there's tremendous influence at that point." Therefore, according to this study's findings, the professor wields the bulk of the influence, good or bad, in the student's life. That said, the study revealed that more than giving access is needed. Communication must be personal to achieve this transformational and inspirational level of connection, but it must also be timely.

Self-Leadership Practice 2: Prompt Feedback. Two major factors contributing to feelings of isolation in online students pertain to the timing and content of feedback the students receive on their assignments and questions about them. For Participant 16, prompt and personal feedback was "vital to the student's success, not just academically, but emotionally, mentally, just staying in a healthy place. One of the difficulties of my [online educational experience] was when professors who were not checking in or engaged just completely went M.I.A." That is why, Participant 9 says, "I always make it a practice to respond within 24 hours. Suppose a student tries to contact me. It is usually much sooner than that because I always check my email, but at most, it is 24 hours." Consequently, Participant 6 admonished all online professors that "in an ideal world, a student would never get back a paper without some kind of personal comment, as opposed to A.P.A. or formatting errors, those things being highlighted. An ideal online educational experience will convince the students that they are not just working with A.I." Participant 12 agreed, "I think having that connection with the professor can give you some context to whatever you are studying. We are not just asking you to grade and be in discussion forms. We want you to share your unique experiences. I think that it not only makes things more enjoyable for the instructor, but it also makes things more enjoyable for the student." For Participant 17, the majority of professors "communicated often and responded right away," and this greatly enhanced the online learning experience, made participant 17 feel valued, and reduced feelings of anxiety and isolation.

Self-Leadership Practice 3: Curators of Class Culture. The findings have made clear that the responsibility for cultivating a healthy class culture is primarily upon the professor. Participant 13 says, "Well, I think it is on the professor. They are responsible for creating the kind of community they want. Moreover, the truth is it takes more work to build community." Words that participants used to describe this kind of healthy community included collaboration, vulnerability, nurturing, inspiration, understanding, and encouragement. The study revealed that very few people in the student's life can influence and inspire like a fully engaged professor. Participant 1 highlights this point and states, "I think that you ought to be professionally motivated enough to know that and have common sense enough to know that there are limits to the kinds of influence you can have by just communicating and facilitating the learning content. You just need to be more motivated to see your students as more than a consumer of information. Moreover, part of nurturing their full potential goes to understanding the context in which they learn, the motivations which they learn, the barriers to learning that they may have so that you can facilitate the learning experience with greater effectiveness." According to the study, this kind of healthy online learning can only happen if the online professor has a built-in personal solid discipline. The following section will list several healthy self-leadership practices offered by the participants.

Self-Leadership Practice 4: A Disciplined Schedule. The following is a summation of regular daily and weekly exercises from ten of the participants who are actively teaching online classes.

Participant 1 noted the importance of "regularly updated auxiliary resources for the students to support the key unit content."

Participant 3 kept "a journal for each class that I would update after each class on areas to improve on, challenges I had, and what worked well." Additionally, Participant 3 followed a strict schedule of grading assignments and prep for live stream classes.

Participant 5 "set aside time each day to complete assignments, and I sometimes used the spreadsheets provided to organize assignment due dates."

Participant 6 asked when to "interact on discussion boards, grade assignments, etc."

Additionally, Participant 6 "sought to answer emails within 24 hours."

Participant 7 "set blocks of time on certain days aside to complete the work."

Participant 8 stated, "It is my nature to set up the structure, boundaries, calendar reminders, lists of assignments and dates due. Holding myself accountable comes naturally to me."

Participant 9 selected "approximately 1/3 of the students each week to respond to their discussion posts. "I track it so that the next week, it will be a different third, etc., so by week 3, I interacted with each student. Moreover, I never go more than one day without checking on the class and starting to review discussions and assignments as they come in. That way, the students get grades back promptly."

Participant 11 made it a point to regularly communicate on the community dashboard with students to remove as much ambiguity as possible. Participant 11 would go to the L.M.S. site each weekday to go over the site, check for student messages, and respond promptly. Participant 11 says, "Communication is vital for online students and teachers. It is a two-way street." Furthermore, Participant 11 is more than willing to be redundant sometimes to ensure clarity in communication.

Participant 12 says, "I employed regular student-professor communication in my courses (i.e., course week introduction emails, short videos overviewing the weekly content to give some reasons about the content's importance, course week conclusion videos summarizing what had come up in discussion forums/weekly assignments), I gave personalized, actionable feedback to students (i.e., recorded video feedback, written feedback that engaged their work through), and I invested a good amount of time of interacting with students in the discussion forums (i.e., recording video responses, referring them to resources to dive deeper, encouraging students to interact with each other)."

Participant 13 reiterated the importance of staying "on schedule and keeping an accurate record of course dates, times, and media." He said, "I have had to block out large amounts of time to ensure I met deadlines."

The research shows that when these online professors regularly maintained the abovementioned disciplines, the learning experiences for all involved improved dramatically. However, one final group that must be emphasized regarding relational responsibilities is the students. Even if the administration has fully equipped and trained the professors to perform all the practices mentioned above perfectly, the students remain obligated to avail themselves of the relational opportunities before them. Administrators and professors may row their oars in perfect synchrony, but if students do not pick up their own "oars" (responsibilities), the boat will not finish well.

STUDENT RESPONSIBILITY

Participants 2, 4, 6, 7, 8, 12, and 13 stressed the importance of the online student and their responsibilities in building meaningful relationships with their peers and professors. There is little doubt that knowledge and information can be adequately disseminated through remote online means. However, the findings of this study suggest that there is a higher level of learning when that information can be processed in the context of a solid educational community of peers and professors. Participant 7 encourages online learners to "Build the relationships. You will grow more; you will learn more. So, some of that is the professor's initiative. Some of that could be your peer's initiative. However, let me say the vast majority is going to be you." Participant 6 makes it priority one at the beginning of each class to encourage the group to "find someone in your class that you feel like you might be able to connect with and then reach out to them to ask for permission to swap contact information, start some conversation." There is a tremendous short-term benefit when this takes place for the student when they take this initiative. For example, participant 12 highlighted that "the people who are your peers now as you are going through your program, those are going to be peers in the vocation later on." One of the clearest items that emerged from the interviews and journal entries is the belief that friendships play a significant role in taking a student over the finish line in school and keeping them in their prospective callings/professions later. However, if the students do not avail themselves of the opportunities before them, there is little that the administration or professors can do about it. Participant 8 states, "If a student is using online to be able to hide somewhere, that is a different story. However, if they want to get the full experience they need for their educational experience, they will need to connect with others." Participants 2, 6, and 8 concur, stating, "A student really has to make an effort. The burden of this the onus is on the student. It [personal effort] has to be added by the student."

Students have already articulated complaints in previous sections regarding feelings of social isolation caused by what appeared to be disengaged and distracted professors. However, teachers share that there are times when everything has lined up just right for students to connect, and the students still have not taken advantage of the opportunity. Participant 6 laments, "I would offer an hour each night where as many students as want to could come and join me on Zoom, and I will share a little bit about the class, myself, my heart and get to know everybody. I was quickly disappointed by how few people did it and how few came. Nevertheless, for those that did, our online mediated relationship definitely had a different ethos. For the rest of the course, I think I felt more of a connection to them." Participant 7 agreed when they stated, "But what you may be surprised with just making yourself available says something in only a fraction, less than 5% of the students are going to take advantage of it, maybe 2%." Therefore, the frustration arising from disconnected students is not only felt by the students. Online professors have created chances for students to get to know one another only to see the student squander the opportunity. According to Participant 13, "by and large, the student has to initiate the conversation." Though the entire burden of responsibility to create meaningful interactions in an online class does not rest upon one group, the study found that when administration, professors, and students do their parts, friendships are far more likely to transpire in an online class.

Three primary groups emerged as having a shared responsibility for making friends and connections in an online classroom: Administrators, Educators, and Students. Throughout the study, I sought to discover exactly *who* was responsible for facilitating the connection between learners and their leaders. Observing the remarkable openness and careful consideration with which each participant responded was refreshing. Instead of blaming one group or another, each participant swiftly looked introspectively at themselves and articulated how they could have personally done better at facilitating healthy connections. Should one group fail to uphold their duties to the academic or relational process, peer and professor connections may fail to materialize, and the school's overall goals may suffer.

According to the findings, it is ultimately the administration's responsibility to fully outline expectations, provide accountability, train and equip their teams with the necessary tools and rules of relational engagement, empower professors to act creatively, remain flexible and innovative, and potentially the most important of all, they must model healthy relationships between themselves and their teams. Secondly, the teacher is responsible for curating the class culture and maximizing the tools their administrators provide. Being accessible, quick to respond, offering clear and concise communications, and being gracious, helpful, and understanding were qualities outlined by the participants as most conducive to forming healthy connections. Furthermore, it is the responsibility of the students to avail themselves of the resources provided to them by the above groups and take the initiative in making connections. The first two groups can do their jobs perfectly, but if students do not take advantage of the opportunities before them, their overall educational experiences are downgraded significantly.

As mentioned at the beginning of the chapter, the 9-man rowing team representing the U.S.A. from Washington was the best in the world *only* when they all did their part in unity. If even one rower lost focus, the entire boat suffered. A 9-man rowing team only won when they worked in perfect harmony. According to the findings of this study, the same is true of online education. Administrators, Professors, and Students must row in unity. They're all in the same boat, and they only win by working together.

DISCUSS & JOURNAL

DISCUSSION

This chapter outlines responsibilities pertaining to creating a relational culture in the online classroom. <u>The three groups include:</u> students, professors, and administrators. In your journal, write out why you agree with or disagree with the responsibilities outlined in this chapter. Can you think of some that were not listed that should have been?

Other questions to consider with your team...
- How well does your current school operate in unity between departments?
- Do the administration/staff and professors realize that they win only when they work together?
- In your current school, do these three groups exist in their own individual silos or are they in the same boat pulling together to achieve success?

JOURNAL

_____

_____

_____

_____

_____

_____

_____

_____

_____

CHAPTER 4

COMMUNICATION WITHIN THE ONLINE LEARNING COMMUNITY

Let your speech always be gracious, seasoned with salt, so that you may know how you ought to answer each person.

COLOSSIANS 4:6 (ESV)

It was said of the Plains Indians of Montana that they had no greater fear than that of a forest fire. In 1949, one such fire broke out in Mann Gulch, Montana, that would make national headlines and become the subject of study for years to come. A newly formed team of 15 Smoke Jumpers parachuted to combat the blaze, led by a man named Wagner Dodge. When they landed, the conditions on the ground were much worse than they first realized. A foul wind blew the fire forward at 600+ feet a minute, far faster than most people can run. The team of 15 brave souls was trapped between the high bluffs of the gorge and a raging, rapidly approaching blaze. Within moments, all the smoke jumpers knew that hope of surviving this fire was all but gone as a wall of flame, nearly 30 feet high, crashed down upon them. [1] What happened next surprised everyone. As a very unlikely door of escape began to reveal itself.

The leader remained calm and had an idea. Realizing they would lose the race against the fire, their team leader decided to light his own fire. Dodge stopped, lit a matchbook, and threw it at his feet. It burned up all of the debris and grass around him. His logic was that if he burned up all of the fuel around himself, he'd be safe when the fire attempted to overtake him because there was nothing left for it to burn. This technique later became known as an escape fire. In the weeks to follow, an investigation was done to see how he was able to escape. When asked why he started the fire, Dodge said, "I started the fire to take refuge in the fire."

I wish that I could say that the story had a happy ending, but unfortunately, Dodge and two others, who had miraculously found sanctuary among some rocks, were the only survivors. He tried his best to communicate to his team to jump into the escape fire with him, but no one listened. It did not matter how frantically he signaled or how loudly he screamed. His team assumed that he was experiencing a panic-induced mental breakdown and decided to take their chances at outrunning the fire. Dodge had a brilliant idea, and that idea has become standard training for those in the forest rescue service; however, while it is true that the escape fire method has been saving lives ever since, in the heat of the moment, the best idea was rejected by the team because it had never been done before. If his team had listened to him, all 15 jumpers would likely have survived the day with little harm, but unfortunately, they did not. [2]

Was Dodge the team leader? Yes, he was. His position, rank, and previous experience suggest that everyone in the group should obey his orders. Was Dodge clear about what he wanted the team to do? Yes, he was. They all understood what he was saying. He was telling them to join him in the fire. His message could not have been any clearer. **But just because someone has positional leadership over a group and that leader has a clear message does not guarantee that people will follow, especially if the leader's directives are unknown or unproven.** The historical account of the Mann Gulch Fire has a particularly relevant lesson for us concerning the importance of communication. More specifically, not only the means but also the timing of communication.

As previously mentioned, the smoke jump team was a newly formed unit with no previous experience fighting fires *together*. The leader, Wagner Dodge, was undoubtedly the most knowledgeable and experienced one of the group. Still, some had never fought a fire before this moment and had only been through a several-week training course. One might argue that the men who passed away were casualties of a system that did not allow for much prior communication and camaraderie between the leader and the rest of the team. The less experienced members did not have an opportunity to build rapport with or benefit from the years of wisdom that resided in their leader. Due to this communication vacuum, it appears that the positional rank of the leader was not strong enough to influence a following when it really mattered.

In most of my ten years of online education, I met my classmates and teachers for the first time at the beginning of a semester. There was no previous communication or ability to build rapport with or benefit from the collective wisdom that resided in the professor or fellow students. The class is a newly assembled group with zero to no previous experience with each other. An online class has a leader with positional authority and influence. They are the leader due to their years of expertise, experience, and education in their prospective field. However, many online communication systems are not set up so that the student can mine out the great benefit of the leader's know-how. Many systems of communication need to be built to help the professor advance beyond a positional/title form of leadership and become a transformational influence in the pupils' lives. One of the primary goals of a *remotely close* classroom is to address this problem by offering practical and readily applicable solutions to the communication issues in online education.

RELATIONAL & ACADEMIC COMMUNICATION

Within the following section, I aim to answer the question of communication, specifically, the question of timing, what should be communicated, and when it should be communicated within the calendar of an online class. Many participants felt that this is the primary area of focus to either prevent or cause a sense of social isolation and its varying forms of anxiety and stress. For this study, the timeline of one online class is broken down into three parts: the pre-start of class, the start of class, and post-class communication. These three sections articulate what the participants of this study felt should be communicated before class begins, during class, and after the class is finished to help all involved be better connected. As previously mentioned, communication is not a one-way street; therefore, administrators, teachers, and students alike all contribute to the overall success of excellent and timely communication.

PRE-START OF CLASS

An escape fire was thought to be a brand-new method of rescue in 1949, but the tragedy of the Mann Gulch incident brought to light the fact that the Plains Indians had used that method to survive prairie fires like this one for generations. [3] The information was available long before the life-taking event with Dodge's team occurred. As they say, hindsight is 20/20, and it is very easy for spectators to sit in judgment of what could have been done to avoid the loss of life, but the fact remains: a viable solution had existed for generations; why was it only after the Mann Gulch Fire that it became a mainstream method of survival training? It has been argued that if there had been adequate training and communication *prior* to the fire jumpers leaving the plane, they would have likely survived, and they would not have assumed that their leader had lost his mind by building a fire of his own, which brings us to the first point of this section. It is essential, vital even, to communicate clearly prior to the start of class to avoid the fires of needless conflict and social isolation.

Ideally, according to the findings of this study, good communication between online professors and their students must begin long before day one of the class. Participant 12 reiterates this point: "An ideal online class starts with the professor proactively reaching out to the students before the class begins, welcoming them, getting them ready so that nothing catches them off guard so that there is a good start to that course." As soon as contact information is made available to the online professor, sending informal correspondence offering prayer, encouragement, and scriptural devotional thoughts can add substantial relational value, according to Participant 11. At a minimum, and if at all possible, according to Participant 12, "the professor is reaching out a month before class begins," introducing him or herself, letting them know what books or other resources are needed for the course, and anything else that they may need to alleviate anxiety and helping them to understand what it takes to be successful in the course.

START OF CLASS

Within moments of Dodge and the other jumpers landing in the fire zone, the team separated from their leader, and communication did not occur between the group and Dodge for some time. At the very beginning of their fight against the blaze, when communication was most needed, it was nowhere to be found. Leaving the team to wonder what the best plan of attack was and, more importantly, what the plan to get out alive was. A communication breakdown ultimately led to tragedy at this critical juncture in the mission. Leaders must communicate well before the beginning of an effort, and to keep the positive momentum in the future, connecting and reconnecting again and again at the start is paramount.

In Participant 14's experience, this is the stage in the timeline that they felt the most socially isolated. Participant 14 "felt socially isolated" due to a lack of understanding regarding all aspects of the class and not knowing who the first point of contact would be should there be a problem. Participant 14 went on to say, "I did feel separated. I felt like I did not know who to turn to or who to talk to. I was even very insecure about what I got myself into." One of the first priorities for Participant 9, when they teach an online class, is to "have a live session with the students" via an online streaming portal like Zoom or Google Meet. Doing this has allowed Participant 9 "to connect with them more personally, as opposed to just a faceless name in the course as the professor." To add another point of value to the social connection and corresponding support throughout the class experience, Participant 6 would like to see a peer mentor assigned to this point in the class timeline that follows them through every single part of the course so that collaborative conversations can more easily transpire. Participant 6 said, "If there were some way that programs across the board could either require that or provide that, man, that would be gold."

DURING CLASS

Once the team regrouped with their leader, they knew that whatever their original mission was, it had changed. The goal at this point was to get out alive. Dodge ordered his team to leave behind their equipment and follow him as quickly as possible. Amid the inferno, basic survival instincts began taking hold of the team. The more they ran, the more separated they became from one another and, more importantly, their leader. Once they finally caught up to Wagner and saw him motioning them to join him in the escape fire, communication had been lost so long that they ignored him and made their own plans. Thus, the next point is that the leader must not only start well but also continue to be *consistently* in touch with their class so that the multiple challenges of social isolation can be navigated healthily.

For Participant 15, feelings of social isolation and disconnection were most strongly felt after the class had begun. "Sometimes I think people do not exist on the other side of a screen." Admittedly, participant 15 is a natural-born introvert, and one of the main reasons for choosing to gain an education online was for the "benefit" of not having to deal too much with people. However, once the class began, this natural-born, self-proclaimed introvert began to feel that something from the educational experiences needed to be improved. Participant 15 recalled, "I prided myself on being a huge introvert, so I love being alone. However, I realized I was missing something after getting into it [online class]. I felt a missing connection with the people I was learning with." According to the findings, the solution to this problem is constant, timely, and personal communication. Participant 4, 5, 8, 9, and 12 all reiterated their practice of keeping an email or voicemail from going unanswered beyond 24 hours. Participant 8 recalled the most aggravating thing about online professors being those who would not respond quickly, wouldn't interact, and appeared indifferent to their students. When reasonable, timely, and personalized communication is taking place, general feelings of being valued, recognized, and appreciated are mentioned by several participants. Participant 6 states that every successful online professor must "always seek to add a personal touch to every touch point," be it grading comments, bulk emails, or announcements.

POST CLASS

After the fire had died out and the smoke had cleared, 12 of the 15 smoke jumpers were gone, and three remained to debrief with leaders from various organizations. They evaluated each other, constructively criticized themselves, and learned from their mistakes. A post-fire review of the situation has led to better processes and leadership development for fire and rescue teams for the last many decades. Were mistakes made during the Mann Gulch situation? The three survivors believed so, and we benefit from those honest evaluations. This leads me to my final thoughts on this matter. No one believed they had performed flawlessly as an online educational leader in the study of previously published literature or in my pool of participants. Therefore, the research suggests that it is only through the ability to access and learn from honest feedback and post-class reviews that we may evaluate our mistakes and continue to improve.

Two leader group participants, who have had many years of online teaching and administrative experience, highlighted the importance of a post-class debrief or review. Participant 6 stated, "I need to have a sense that I am influencing, encouraging, and lifting up people. Moreover, the only way to get that sense is through feedback that comes through the relational feedback cycle." It is typical for professors to receive a post-class survey review from their students that semester; however, if the professors are not given access to that information, they cannot benefit or improve. Participant 13 states, "On a professional level, the professor gains feedback from students regarding the effectiveness of her or his teaching method based on the conversations they have with students outside the minimum requirements." Based on the study's findings, there was a general sense that more conversations between administration, fellow teachers, and students were regularly desired to innovate and continually improve the online course.

The circumstances on the ground of Mann Gulch in 1949 were far different than they first appeared when looking down from the plane thousands of feet in the air. The distance was too great for the smoke jumpers to comprehend the depth of danger they were about to enter. Only after they were on the ground feeling the wind-whipped heat of the fire against their faces did they understand for themselves just how vulnerable they were to being overcome by the blaze. However, once they landed, there was no retreat; they had to adapt to the situation or encounter terrible consequences. Tragically, the communication necessary for successfully achieving their goal was handicapped by the very system in which they had trained and worked. It is my prayer that the same could never be said of us. For a *remotely close* classroom to succeed, it will be marked by a communication system that values and prioritizes constant connection with all parties involved. This will significantly help us, as educators, mitigate social isolation's destructive flames.

DISCUSS & JOURNAL

DISCUSSION

For this journal entry, think of and list as many possible steps that could be made to improve communication in your school.

JOURNAL

_____

_____

_____

_____

_____

_____

_____

_____

_____

_____

_____

_____

_____

_____

_____

CHAPTER 5

OPPORTUNITIES FOR BUILDING ONLINE LEARNING COMMUNITIES

Look carefully then how you walk, not as unwise
but as wise, making the best use of the time.

EPH. 5:15-16 (ESV)

I n the winter of 1903, children playfully gathered along the tops
of the dunes of Kitty Hawk, North Carolina, hoping to catch a
glimpse of two out-of-towners who periodically set up camp along
the shore to watch and mimic the birds. Not only did the children find
entertainment in this awkward diversion to their otherwise predictable
lives, but these brothers from Ohio received more than one odd look
from the grown-ups. It must have been quite a thing to behold as two
respectable-looking men spent their every waking moment facing the
nearly constant wind with outstretched arms running and bending
and turning along the beach as though they expected to suddenly join
the friendly fowl in the air. To the untrained eye, these men appeared
to be more than a little off, but they were studying how to harness the
power of wind.

The Wright Brothers are credited with inventing the first ever fully
operational manned airplane. They were the sons of a local church

pastor and had built a very successful bicycle shop in Dayton, Ohio. Though they displayed an evident aptitude for mechanics and business, nothing about their family background or formal education would have officially qualified them for aeronautics. Yet, Orville and Wilbur Wright became obsessed with leaving the earth behind to enjoy God's creation from Heaven's perspective. They were determined to fly, but to do so, they needed "to be on intimate terms with the wind." [1]

Just as the Wright Brothers needed to find a geographical location that would provide the requisite environment for test flights, the online student must be afforded relational online opportunities by their professors if they are to truly soar to the heights of their academic and professional potential. What follows are the findings of my research that, when put together, form the needed relational atmosphere for the student to gain friendships and the corresponding benefits thereto.

RELATIONAL & ACADEMIC OPPORTUNITIES

The proceeding approaches were gleaned from the participants' interviews and journal entries. They felt these were the top 5 methods that would foster relationships in the online classroom. They include online office hours, optional online social times, synchronistic class time, written and video discussion boards, and optional opportunities for in-person meet-ups. Each of these approaches saw varying amounts of success in the online class based on administrators, professors, or students' willingness to enact the previously mentioned responsibilities. It must be noted that the findings reveal that each of these sub-categories was suggested not by any individual group but all groups. This means that each sub-category is viewed in a positive light by each group of participants. Furthermore, they were recommended practices for a better online educational experience.

ONLINE OFFICE HOURS

Around the turn of the 20th century, the Wright brothers wrote a letter to the U.S. Weather Bureau in Washington, DC, to enquire about a location that would provide all the needed environmental dynamics to conduct their flight experiments safely. The first and most crucial element required would be a place with strong, constant, and predictable wind. For without the wind, there was no hope of success. Just as the Wright brothers needed a strong, steady, and predictable wind to fly, the online student must have access to a strong, constant, and available professor. The study revealed that student academic success suffers tremendously without this element in place.

For the online student, the study revealed that having regularly scheduled online office hours significantly alleviated feelings of isolation. Participants 6 and 7 strongly suggested virtual office hours. Alternatively, as Participant 8 recommends, "I will just open my Zoom Room, and it will be open for 30 minutes every day." This creates a relaxed online environment for students to "pop in" and out at their convenience to ask quick questions about assignments or to benefit from personal mentorship moments. Participant 3 says, "You are not just a professor but a mentor. Furthermore, one of the greatest joys is speaking into the lives of young men and women and those who are not so young in their calling and [sharing] life lessons that I have learned over the years. As a professor, I think you are so much more than just somebody who is regurgitating knowledge you have learned over the years in a sterile environment."

The findings of this study reveal that having regularly scheduled virtual office hours is a tool that both students and professors alike have come to appreciate. Not only does it help academically, but participants noted that the relational connection was at another level for those who took advantage of this tool. The importance of holding consistent and predictable times when the students can gain access to the professor cannot be overstated. It is the student's "Kitty Hawk." This is where they find the needed wind to soar, but scheduled online office hours are only the first of five recommendations. The next four are equally vital.

OPTIONAL ONLINE SOCIAL TIMES

In addition to having a place with constant wind, the Wrights needed a place that would allow them to observe birds-a-plenty. These aeronautical novices reasoned that the only way to learn how to fly would be through meaningful interaction and the up-close study of birds. Kitty Hawk was the perfect place for these budding ornithologists. Orville Wright would say, "Learning the secret of flight from a bird was a good deal like learning the secret of magic from a magician." Nearly any kind of bird one might think of was in regular attendance at Kitty Hawk. Eagles, hawks, vultures, pigeons, and white gannets seemed to fill the sky, and the Wright brothers couldn't write in their journals fast enough all of the amazing things they learned from the "miracle of birds." While it may be true that the Wrights were simply laymen regarding flight, their common-sense approach of being close to creatures who knew how to fly paid off in huge ways. In the same way, the study before you reveals that students learn more the nearer they are relationally with fellow students and professors. Therefore, creating space for these connections to happen only makes sense.

No one can force another person into an authentic friendship. Participants agreed that the best a leader can do is curate the online environment and make it as conducive as possible for connection. "Online learning can be very lonely. Furthermore, one of the values of in-person learning that we have yet to figure out how to encourage in online learning would be that of the collegial atmosphere, meaning the collaboration and the relationships students are given," says Participant 6. It is otherwise noted by Participant 3 that one of the significant benefits of a person's college career is having the opportunity to mingle with people from different cultures regularly. There is potential, Participant 3 notes, for this to happen at an even greater level with online learning if teachers create informal optional social times and glean "insights from others who have such a different worldview." As Participant 8 says, "The most valuable relationship is going to be to connect with someone that's taking the same subject you are at the same time you are."

However, according to Participant 2, it is the student's decision "to engage each other, especially in informal ways. That is the foundation. Participant 15 called for a "virtual lounge" or "virtual happy hour" where class members could connect simultaneously over a Zoom call to get better acquainted, especially at the beginning of the course. The study's interesting and somewhat unexpected finding is expressed in the next section: administrators, teachers, and students all agree that their online experience would have a greater sense of social connection if there were a few live/required online class times during the semester. As Participant 7 says, students must be given "chances to interact, to build relationships." The Wright Brothers had to get close to the birds to learn the secret of flying. The same is true of online students. To gain the full benefit of wisdom that their educational journey can provide, they need to get as close as possible to one another.

SYNCHRONISTIC CLASS TIME

Kitty Hawk, NC, provided the needed wind patterns and all the birds one could want, but that would not have been enough all by itself; the Wrights needed something more. They needed the help of the locals. Luckily for Orville and Wilbur, they found the residence of Kitty Hawk more than amenable to their needs. Little more than 50 modestly built rustic homes dotted the arid landscape. Their occupants were the descendants of those who had shipwrecked upon the islands and never left. They farmed and hunted what they could, but they primarily availed themselves of the year-round fishing to make ends meet. They lived simply, off of the provision of the land and sea, just as their ancestors had before them. It is said of the people that they "believed in a good God, a bad devil, a hot hell and more than anything else they believed that same God never intended for humans to ever fly."

Though their belief system differed significantly from that of the Wright Brothers with regard to human flight, they greatly admired the work ethic of the Wrights, and so they were "consistently friendly and desirous to help." The next piece of the puzzle that would allow for the Wrights to succeed was learning to work with new people, even ones who didn't necessarily agree with what they were attempting to do. They found common ground. The research findings outlined in this section show that it is through synchronistic online class time that the same working dynamic can be best accomplished.

Participants 6, 7, 13, and 15 highly recommended synchronistic online class time to advance better online educational experiences. Participant 6 stated, "In an ideal world, I would love for there to be requirements for synchronous [online classes]. Students must be together online, not in person, but at least synchronous connections, whether once a week or once every two weeks. Furthermore, Participant 6 said, "I almost want to put an asterisk next to an online degree. Not that it is any less work and any less valid in terms of that, but as far as the holistic life-shaping value, unless you, like I even said before, have friends that you can talk to and process with what you are learning, I think you are missing out." Participant 13 agrees, "I think that the ideal online education experience is where you have multiple students in a live forum online where they get to interact with each other and the professor...a mix between live education and recorded lectures on scene." Participant 15, a self-proclaimed introvert stated, that it would be a huge improvement to online education to have "a combination of both" [synchronistic and asynchronistic] class time. While it may take a little extra effort for professors to create these opportunities, the long-term relational and educational benefits appear well worth it. Participant 7, someone with over a decade of online teaching experience, excitedly stated, "Let's get on live; let's do some live interaction."

If it were not for the assistance of the local population at Kitty Hawk, it is unlikely that the Wrights would have succeeded in their initial experiments. They had to work in a group to maximize their efforts, but that was not all. As we will see in the next section, flying was (and still is) a dangerous enterprise. Defying the safety of gravity was to take one's life in hand and risk injury or even death. This is why the Wrights made it their practice never to fly together so that in the event of a fatal crash, one brother would still be alive to carry on their work. Therefore, the Wright brothers would need a safe (and soft) landing area in case of an unexpected wreck.

WRITTEN AND VIDEO DISCUSSION BOARDS

With regards to actually taking flight, Wilbur Wright noted, "The chief need was skill rather than machinery. It was impossible to fly with both knowledge and skill – and skill came only from experience." There was a significant problem, however, that of safety. When the Wrights wrote the U.S. Weather Bureau to gain advice for a very particular location conducive to their needs, there was one that was an absolute must if they intended to return home in one piece – they needed a soft landing pad. So far, Kitty Hawk checked all the boxes. If there was one thing these islands of the Outer Banks had, it was sand – and lots of it. This would allow the Wrights to gain knowledge through practical experimentation, thus gaining the skill to fly. In the same way that the Wrights needed a safe landing zone, online students must be granted a safe space to throw around their ideas and gain the insights of others. The research findings identified two ways to accomplish just that: written and video discussion boards.

Though there were mixed feelings about the effectiveness of discussion board posts from all participating groups, no one felt it was time to do away with them entirely. Instead, most felt that they still play a vital role in the socialization of students and disseminating information if all fully maximize them. As Participant 5 puts it, "Well, I think one of the reasons we wanted not to eliminate the discussion board was because we wanted students and professors to be able to interact and provide that sense of community within their coursework. We want the mentorship. There is a sense of responsibility. These are not just students who are taking the course. We want them to be mentored." Participant 4 agreed and said, "Yeah, I think that part of that ideal experience would be that the discussion board conversations would be provocative and truly engage people's lives, not just the content." One suggestion to innovate and update the discussion board experience that several participants brought out was to add a video discussion component. Participant 4 stated, "I was excited to learn that the LMS included a way to integrate Zoom in the classroom so that professors who want to do that can add that aspect because it does bring another level." Participants 7 and 8 agreed that discussion boards can "facilitate that relational connection" and "gives opportunity for [the student] even to know who [their] peers are." Adding recorded video discussions rather than a required written word count may add another valuable relational and learning component.

To make discussion boards work the intended way, the study suggests offering clearly articulated boundaries and expectations regarding respect, kindness, and openness at the outset of class. For these discussion boards to really accomplish something special in a learner's life, they must feel their ideas have a "safe/soft landing pad" upon which to fall. Otherwise, the best a professor can expect is superficial interaction that is just enough to gain a passing grade.

So far, Kitty Hawk has delivered on the need for wind to catch, birds to observe, helpful and friendly people, and a soft landing pad. But there is one last item on the Wright brother's list of needs – the ability to work in solitude as long as they needed until they were ready to show the world what they had created.

OPTIONAL IN-PERSON MEET-UPS

The Wright Brothers' father was a local church pastor, and they were the proud owners of a local bike shop in Dayton, Ohio. They were undoubtedly grounded in the principles of faith and family, and with their active minds, they built a successful and popular business. That said, one thing that the Wright family was not was wealthy. Therefore, it was going to take time, patience, and a little bit of anonymity to create their aircraft. When the season for selling bicycles ended, they boarded up their shop windows and began to work out the dynamics of their flying machine. Not only did it need to be built in secret, it would need to be tested in secret. Doing this would protect their designs from the all too willing thieves of the day. Considering the enormous wealth and notoriety available to the first-to-fly, it is no wonder so many were racing for this particular finish line. The commercial and military applications of flight were limitless. This fact alone made it very important for the Wright brothers to pick their moment well as to when they would reveal their creation to the world. A temporary season of solitude was needed, and Kitty Hawk gave them all they wanted and more. Once they were ready to go public with their flying machine, they could emerge from the wind-swept dunes – but not before.

Often, it is the convenience, accessibility, and relative anonymity of online education that entices many with an introverted or shy nature to seek out such learning options. This personality type is represented among the study participants, and they even expressed a desire to emerge from their solitude to interact with their classmates once they felt ready to do so. While it is true that they liked having a season of solitude, they also suggested that it would be nice for the option of in-person meet-ups to be made available once they achieved a level of comfort with others in the class. At times, in the natural course of the introductory section of an online class, members discover that they live near one another. In those cases, one participant, number 14, actually arranged for an impromptu coffee shop study group. As a result, participant 14 said, "It benefited my educational experience to have some in-person connection." Participants 1, 2, 4, and 6 shared the same vantage point: "The online was much richer because I had those in-person experiences."

At the same time, it may not be possible nor allowed to make in-person gatherings a required element of online learning; most felt it should be an optional benefit whenever possible. Participant 1 states that the optimal online classroom delivery system includes "solid content that is delivered in an organized way, reinforcement of that content with learning experiences that are done in small group settings." According to Participant 2, for this to work, "I think it rises and falls with the student commitment and the amenities made available by the school and by the professor." Just as the Wrights needed time to work out their experiments and build their confidence before they made themselves available to a broader audience, the online student may desire the option to connect with a wider group once they have built their confidence to do so.

This chapter discussed the opportunity within the online classroom to make more excellent social connections with classmates and professors. It answers the questions of where and when. As exemplified by the lives of the Wright Brothers, who needed a specific type of location to learn to fly, the online student must be similarly afforded optional times and places for social connection by the school they attend. Orville and Wilbur knew that to safely leave behind the earth to join the birds in the air, they would need a place with constant wind, lots of birds to learn from, a helpful populace, a safe landing zone, and privacy. Each of these items has served as an illustration of the five overarching needs of the online student. Just as the Wrights needed Kitty Hawk, the online learner needs a school to provide the requisite ethos for the student to soar to their potential.

At the close of this chapter, I would like to leave you with one final thought. Though Kitty Hawk offered the perfect circumstances for the Wrights to achieve their goals, it does not mean that these islands were without their challenges. The wind, for example, became a double-edged sword. On the one hand, the wind was needed for their experiments, but it was also very dangerous. More than once, Orville and Wilbur were awakened at night by the wind sweeping their entire camp away into the darkness. If they were not being assaulted by bed bugs, wood insects, or sand gnats, they had to ward off clouds of countless thousands of mosquitos that were so thick it is said they could "darken the sun." Unpredictable temperatures were a constant concern, as it could be unbearably hot during the day and freezing at night. The point that I am making is that even the perfect locations have their own set of unique obstacles to overcome. The same is true as it relates to creatively thinking outside the norm to find new ways of bringing online learners and leaders together for each other's mutual benefit. It will take hard work, humility, collaboration, and a willingness to face great challenges – but in the end, if we persevere, we will soar.

DISCUSS & JOURNAL

DISCUSSION QUESTIONS

In this journal entry, write down the ways that you and your team are currently providing opportunities for connection and friendship in the online class. This chapter discussed occasions within the online classroom to make excellent social connections with classmates and professors. It answers the questions of where and when.

Where and when are you currently doing this for your students? How does this need to improve in your context?

JOURNAL

_____

_____

_____

_____

_____

_____

_____

_____

_____

_____

_____

_____

_____

_____

CHAPTER 6
RECOMMENDATIONS FOR POLICY MAKERS AND PRACTITIONERS

Let the wise hear and increase in learning,
and the one who understands obtain guidance.

PROVERBS 1:5 (ESV)

In December of 1912, The Endurance was the finest ship ever built of its kind. With a singular purpose, the most skilled Norwegian shipbuilders carefully and methodically selected each piece of wood and "fitted it with the closest tolerance; every joint and every fitting cross-braced something else for the maximum strength." [1] Today, it would cost well over a million dollars to replicate such a ship, but it was purchased by the famed British explorer Ernest Shackleton for $67,000. Upon purchase, it was officially commissioned to be the vessel that would undertake one of the most daring exploits the world has ever known: The Imperial Trans-Antarctic Expedition. The expedition's goal was to cross the Antarctic continent overland from west to east. To accomplish such a mission, Shackleton would require a ship that could maneuver through and manipulate the floating pack ice of the infamous Weddell Sea. Some of the ice flows were as large as islands and weighed tens of millions of tons. Thus, the name of the ship was quite appropriate, for it would take immeasurable endurance to achieve their goal.

The Endurance was the perfect fusion of the modern technology of the day with proven shipbuilding methods that had been passed down through the generations. It was constructed by the renowned Framnaes Shipyard in Sandefjord, Norway. If you needed a whaling or sealing vessel for the Arctic or Antarctic, there was no one better in the world to commission. Christian Jacobsen, a Framnaes master-builder, supervised the project and "insisted on employing men who were not only skilled shipwrights, but had been to sea themselves in whaling and sealing ships." The Endurance could harness the wind with its three barkentine masts and was supplemented by the power of a coal-fired, 350-horsepower steam engine, giving the Endurance the ability to reach speeds of above 10 knots (just under 12 miles an hour). Though the ship was beautifully and meticulously built by the best possible people, and even though it carried with it the merger of old and new technology, the Endurance would unfortunately not endure. On October 27, 1915, it would come face-to-face with an unexpected force strong enough to splinter its 2-foot-thick sides into millions of fragile toothpicks.

What is a ship but a vehicle to get people from where they are to where they want to be? In this chapter, I'd like to suggest that the Endurance serves as an illustration of what can happen to even the best [educational] vehicle when it encounters powerful and unexpected exterior forces. Online education is a medium employed by countless millions of people to get them from where they are to where they want to be; however, over the last many years, powerful and unexpected forces have applied a great deal of pressure upon all aboard this [educational] ship. One might consider online learning tools as a merger of new technologies with proven educational practices of the past, but the research before us suggests that modifications must be made if we hope to achieve our goals and endure the mounting pressures that threaten success.

A five-fold focus is highlighted in the following section. Informed by the research, recommendations for policymakers and practitioners are made to enable them to adjust their educational sails to better navigate today's online challenges.

(See Appendices 3 & 4 for further reference.)

THE FIVE-FOLD FOCUS FOR ONLINE EDUCATIONAL SUCCESS

This section will underscore the five primary empirical implications of the study. These propositions include 1) the qualities of a great online professor, 2) issues pertaining to learning management systems and technology, 3) the importance of attaining emotional support systems and community, 4) the value of quality communication, and 5) best practices for onboarding processes for new students and new hires. The study fully corroborated previous research while adding spiritual elements that undergird what the participants felt to be the proper motivation behind all of their online educational efforts. Furthermore, this study revealed that when these five educational focuses are fully communicated, understood, and implemented by the three main groups (administrators, teachers, and students), the entire school benefits and is given its best chance to meet or exceed online educational goals. Additionally, the findings show that if even one of these empirical implications is ignored, all passengers in the educational *boat* suffer.

FOCUS #1: QUALITIES OF A GREAT ONLINE PROFESSOR.

Shackleton was not the first nor the last to attempt the seemingly insurmountable task of conquering the vast wasteland of the Antarctic. Two other notable explorers of his day had tried it as well and enjoyed the limelight, Robert F. Scott and Roald Amundsen. These two alphas were engaged in one of the most storied rivalries to be the first to plant their nation's flag at the South Pole. Tragically for Scott, one of the last things he saw before slipping into eternity was the Amundsen's Norwegian flag stiffly flapping in the freezing wind of the Antarctic.

Amundsen had beaten him by one month, and Scott had to settle for second place perpetually. Scott and Amundsen were tremendous leaders in their own right. However, it was said, "For scientific leadership give me Scott; for swift and efficient travel, Amundsen; but when you are in a hopeless situation, when there seems no way out, get down on your knees and pray for Shackleton."

While Shackleton's quest to cross the continent failed, he succeeded at something that may be an even more remarkable accomplishment: his leadership rescued the lives of all 27 members of his crew. Time and space would not permit me to write about the numerous leadership moments that culminated in what is arguably the most incredible survival story in recorded history, but for the purposes of this book, I'll highlight the following. Perce Blackboro, a young Welsh who was a buddy of a few of the crew members, hid himself on the Endurance and remained hidden until the ship was too far out to sea to turn back. When Shackleton discovered him, he was enraged and let loose a torrent of rebuke upon all involved in this conspiracy. Then, Shackleton approached the young stowaway and sternly informed him, "If we run out of food and anyone has to be eaten, you will be first. Do you understand?" The young man nervously cracked a smirk and nodded. With that, Blackboro was added to the ship's log and given the job of cook's mate. Not long after that moment, everyone, including Shackleton, began to view him as a valuable member of the crew.

The point that I'd like to draw from this story is simple. Even though Shackleton was well within his rights to severely punish Blackboro and those who smuggled him aboard, he chose instead to integrate him into the mission of the ship. Shackleton went out of his way to not only lead, encourage, and rescue those that he personally chose for the adventure, but he made a special effort to connect with and encourage even the stowaway. In the end, everyone, from the captain to Blackboro, is saved because Shackleton leads them all with equal love and attention.

With every new class, be it in-person or online, new interpersonal connections between students and their professors will come. While it may be natural for the professor to socially connect easily with some students over others, as a truly called and caring leader of the classroom, the professor will treat everyone with equal attention. The research adds weight to this pivotal point of focus. If the professor pursues all students with frequent and fervent communication, the learner has the best chance of success.

Throughout the literature review, a common informational thread wove its way through it all: that of the professor's perceived and actual attentiveness and availability. The study's findings fully concur with the literature on the point that students must know that the educator is available and present. [2] Participants 6 and 7 highlighted the importance of having and keeping regularly scheduled online office hours. Participants 6, 7, 13, and 15 call for periodic synchronistic class time, which may offer extra time for the professor to engage personally and spiritually. The most essential quality of an online professor, per the literature review and the findings of this study, pertains to engagement. More specifically, the professor goes above and beyond the syllabus to ensure that each student knows they will not be ignored by the teacher.

The theoretical framework shows that there is a healthy relational connection at the foundation of any academic or social solution. According to the findings, quality communication is the solution to students feeling disconnected or isolated. More specifically, it is constant, timely, and personal communication. Feeling the lack of this type of communication was the primary cause of social isolation and its varying forms of anxiety and stress, according to the research. Participant 16 states that this kind of communication is "vital to the student's success, not just academically, but emotionally, mentally, just staying in a healthy place." The study found that when reasonable, timely, and personalized communication is taking place, general feelings of being valued, recognized, and appreciated are experienced by all. That said, the study further reveals that three primary parties must communicate back and forth: administrators, faculty, and students. If any of these groups fail to offer constant, timely, and personal communication, relationships break down; thus further perpetuating the ramifications of social isolation.

The ideal online professor understands and lives out the priority of communicating and reaching the lives of all of their students with equal enthusiasm. Just as Shackleton loved and led the first-in-command as much as the fugitive, the ideal online leaders must offer themselves equally to their students. For this to happen, the online leader must not only have the proper motivation but also attain the needed training to fully maximize the tools at their disposal to achieve the goal. This brings us to the next empirical implication pertaining to the school's LMS.

FOCUS #2: THE LEARNING MANAGEMENT SYSTEM & TECH. CONCERNS.

It was said of Shackleton that he possessed an "indomitable self-confidence and optimism" which had the power to "set men's souls on fire" and just "being in his presence was an experience." One could argue that it was the attitude of the leader that ultimately led to the rescue of the other 27 souls that were in his care. The entire team needed what he had: an undying belief that they would succeed against all odds. Just as Shackleton's good attitude was contagious, there were others in the crew who did not share his positive outlook. The leader of the company knew that if these men with a propensity for pessimism were allowed to spread their ideals, it could have dire consequences. The answer to this problem was that Shackleton put the problematic people in his own tent in hopes of passing on his good attitude to them and protecting the others from negative thoughts.

The point here is that the survival of the crew depended on whether or not Shackleton could give his men what he possessed: an unbeatable and resolute attitude. If the crew could not get what Shackleton had to offer, they would not have what they needed to live. In the same way, the next generation needs what the older generation possesses: years of knowledge, experience, and wisdom. If the next generation does not get what the older generation has to offer them, there could be dire consequences.

Many seasoned teachers sense that the tools used in online classes are very frustrating to learn, hindering them in their efforts to educate. The online delivery systems that they have been given to transfer their vast knowledge to the next generation have actually become a deterrent. Some older educators have actually considered not teaching online classes any longer due to the frustration. This is a devastating finding of the study. Shackleton had the ability to motivate and inspire his men to unthinkable potential because he was unhindered in giving them what he possessed, and if he sensed that something or someone was a potential hindrance, he quickly addressed the problem. The same is true of those who have come before us in education. Older men and women who still have much to offer the next generation can inspire them to higher heights, but what happens if they cannot adequately connect with them due to problematic educational tools? That is what we must consider here.

A non-user-friendly LMS was a common conversational subject in the study. Participant 1 highlighted this point several times and even said that the difficulty of using learning management systems has made him think twice about being involved in online teaching. Furthermore, Participant 1 believed that problematic learning technology is the worst part of online education. Participants 6 and 14 also agree with the literature review that when an LMS is not user-friendly and designed with elements of social connection in mind, the very tool with which the school is attempting to teach becomes a significant deterrent. The findings of the study agree with the literature review that the LMS must be used to create, plan, apply, deliver, and measure learning processes [3] for the delivery of educational content and the communication between professors, students, and peers to be exceptional. [4] Therefore, the following recommendations are made.

Firstly, regular consults should be scheduled between groups for the further improvement of each educational unit. For example, those who create online content should consult with the actual deliverers of that material to the students. This could ensure the online tools are user-friendly and accessible to the teacher. Multiple professors who participated in the study believed a significant disconnect exists between the designers and deliverers of online content. Therefore, it is vital that ongoing conversations between these groups transpire to help older professors feel more comfortable with the technology. Secondly, administrators should consult with students one to two times a semester to ensure that the professor fulfills their agreed-upon social goals for the class. Knowing that these levels of accountability are present may strengthen future relational goals and connections; thereby strengthening the entire school. Participant 6 firmly stated, "In the race to get and keep more students through online courses, universities have sacrificed an essential element of authentic learning – life-on-life influence. Rethinking this should be a high priority." Reevaluating a school's true purpose is paramount as it relates to forming the most effective and efficient modes of online education.

For Christian schools of higher education to truly accomplish the goal of passing on the wisdom, experience, faith, and inspiration of the former generation to the next, their purpose and practice must align. While it is true that not all schools of higher learning have the same mission or purpose, the general principle of aligning one's organizational policy with organizational practice is a transferable concept. As Participant 13 says, "Online education has been around for some time now, but it is still the Wild West when it comes to many institutions." That is why it is vital to bring together all the requisite groups who create and deliver the online material so that there is no hindrance in transferring informational, as well as inspirational, content to the next generation.

Just as it was said of Shackleton, may it also be said of all online educators that we would possess the power to "set men's souls on fire" and inspire them to reach untold potential. To accomplish this goal, another element must be added to the leadership mix. That is, one will need to create a system of social and spiritual support throughout the entire educational experience. Let's turn our attention there now.

FOCUS #3: THRIVING EDUCATIONAL SUPPORT SYSTEMS & COMMUNITY.

In the early days of 1915, the Endurance became surrounded by tremendous and unmoving pack ice. With average temperatures well below zero, hopes of escaping this prison of ice were quickly dashed, and the world's greatest ice-breaking ship itself was broken by frozen floating islands. At this point in the journey, they were still many miles from the mainland, and Shackleton knew that this mission of science was now a mission of survival.

The Endurance was retrofitted to be their new home base of operations while they waited patiently for an opening in the ice that would set them free – an opening that never came. Now that they could not possibly go anywhere, they had to become very intentional in how they kept themselves occupied. There was simply not a lot that they had to do but sit and wait. Shackleton knew that if he did not get creative soon, his men would lose heart. He needed to cultivate a new culture of community and social support to get them through this devastating setback – and that is precisely what he did.

The cargo hold below the main deck, an area of about 875 square feet, became their newly minted living and playing quarters. Everything that had been previously stored there was moved into the old crew's quarters, and this cozy room with wonderfully insulated walls became what they called the Ritz. Books were read aloud; regularly scheduled board games and card games were placed on the calendar. Those men who were educated were booked to share lectures in their various areas of expertise with the rest of the crew. Songs were sung, debates ensued, performances of plays were acted out, and holidays were celebrated. Additionally, in the few hours of the day when sunlight prevailed, hockey games and dog races took place on the very ice that imprisoned their ship. This transformed a potentially deadly situation into one that only reinforced their resolve to live and congealed their comradery.

Creating a community where relationships could be strengthened, and the emotional capacity of the crew could remain healthy was one of the most brilliant leadership moves of all by Shackleton. For the crew to survive, they needed each other, and it is no different for the online educational community. As we will see, the study confirms the tremendous value of a social and spiritual support system marked by a sense of belonging and community within the online classroom.

Embedded within the most successful online educational programs, according to the scholarly literature, is an emotional support system reinforced with academic counselors, mentors, and social coaches. Attaining high levels of trust and mutual support [5] is vital for the online learner. Multiple participants from both sample groups emphasized this point. Participant 9 stresses the importance of encouragement, accountability, and support structures that many online students need while on their educational journey. Participant 12 pointed to the short-term and long-term benefits of these relationships forged during the online college experience and how these relationships carry over into one's professional life. Participants 2, 3, 5, 6, 9, 11, 12, 13, 16, and 17 accentuated the remarkable role that social and spiritual support systems played in their online education. Furthermore, Participant 16 states, "I really think it is vital to the student success, not just academically, but spiritually, emotionally, mentally, just staying in a healthy place." These findings are in sync with the empirical data of the study. However, this study brought out the need for spiritual support systems in addition to the typical social systems that any academic community may offer.

Participant 3 validated this idea and emphasized the importance of the class "feeling as though it is a community" seeking to improve themselves together and "helping each other move along the same path." Participant 5 concurs and stated that one of their primary goals when designing online coursework is for "students and professors to be able to interact and provide that sense of community." About this, Participant 2 stated, "I think it is a step forward to reaching a sort of sense of we are an online educator community" rather than a "scattering" of unknown people. Participant 11 believes that when the school creates opportunities for prayer and devotional time for mutual encouragement through Scripture reading, it becomes the "quickest way to develop community and also to foster the call to why the degree is being taken in the first place." Participant 12 concurs with this notion of shared spirituality when they state, "It was not just an educational process, but a [spiritual] formational process. Moreover, part of Christian formation is being in a Christian community."

Additionally, emotional care support systems must include peer-to-peer mentors, counselors, and coaches. Participant 13 calls for Christian schools to budget for a community care individual that looks out for the social side of things with students, mainly if you are aiming at a young demographic. Participants 3, 4, 5, 6, 13, and 16 all call for varying levels of mentorship to enhance the likelihood of not only achieving academic goals but also doing so without having to experience emotional burnout. Participant 6 argues that every online student should be assigned a peer and professor mentor from the very beginning of their program who could walk with them through every challenge.

When these factors are fully functioning in the life of the student, their sense of belonging and personal inspiration begins to materialize. [6] From the perspective of Participants 6, 7, and 12, these collaborative and collegial environments are critical. The findings concur with the theory, as participants described this healthy community as collaborative, vulnerable, nurturing, inspirational, understanding, and encouraging. A sense of community and belongingness is primarily created by the thoughtful and purposeful professor. [7] For this type of community to exist, a healthy system of communication must be present in the online classroom. Strategies for how this can be accomplished are laid out in the next section. But first, consider that it was a truly masterful leadership move on the part of Shackleton to creatively cultivate so many opportunities for his men to socially support and connect with one another while they were isolated from the rest of the world. Perhaps his wonderful example is something that all of us in educational circles of leadership can emulate.

Thus far, the five-fold focus of leadership has highlighted the qualities of a great online leader, the importance of making connections between those who build the technological tools and those who use them to teach, and creating support systems that build a true sense of belonging and community. Now, we turn our attention to the type of communication that accomplishes these goals.

FOCUS #4: BEST PRACTICES FOR COMMUNICATION

So daunting was the prospect of once again attempting a mission like that of Shackleton and the Endurance that it took more than 40 years before anyone would set out to finish what he started. It was 1957 when Dr. Vivian Fuchs successfully led the Commonwealth Trans-Antarctic Expedition with snow vehicles complete with indoor heating and track wheels. They were equipped with modern radios that could communicate with the outside world and broadcast their exact position in case of an emergency. From the air, they were guided by recon-planes that could inform them of coming obstacles or navigate them onto a better route. Yet, even with these contemporary conveniences, Fuchs' team struggled for more than four months to do what Shackleton had initially set out to achieve. One could argue that the difference between the two teams and ultimate success was technology, but when the situation is distilled to its finest element, the difference between success and failure is isolation. Fuchs' group could contact the outside world and receive help at a moment's notice should the need arise, while Shackleton's crew went for more than a year without any contact with anyone outside of their team. They couldn't have been more isolated unless they were in outer space.

> It was 1915, and there were no helicopters, no Weasels, no Sno-Cats, and no suitable planes. Thus, their plight was naked and terrifying in its simplicity. If they were to get out-they had to get themselves out. [8]

Constant communication and connection made the difference between Fuchs and Shackleton, and it is the key to a successful online educational experience as well.

A commonly shared frustration that both students and professors felt, according to the findings, was a lack of constructive and helpful feedback. Not only do the students need feedback on their assignments so that they may improve upon their skills, but similarly, professors need access to feedback from their students and administrators. Participant 6 stated, "I need to have a sense that I am influencing, encouraging, and lifting people. Moreover, the only way to get that sense is through feedback that comes through the relational feedback cycle." Clearly defined, prompt, expert, impartial, and constant feedback are fundamental to producing superior connections in online courses. [9] In the minds of those studied and documented in the literature, timeliness in grading feedback [10] is one of the most critical aspects of the learning process. All participants in the study agree that this kind of communication is paramount. Furthermore, a recommendation was made for a written and signed agreement between administrators, teachers, and their students. This contract would articulate each other's expectations for the course and highlight best practices for all communication given and received. [11] For example, at the beginning of an online class, when students are checking in, the professor could make it part of the process for students to acknowledge that they have read and understood the appropriate ways to speak with their fellow students and the professor. This would go a long way to avoid future misunderstandings and unnecessary conflict.

As we come now to the final point of our five-fold focus, remember that constant connection and communication were the difference between one explorer's success and another explorer's failure. Because Dr. Fuchs fully maximized the technological tools of his day to remain in constant contact with others, he was able to do something that no one had ever done in the history of the world. May it always be said of us in online education that we are fully exploiting every communicative tool at our disposal to remain in contact with each other so that we can push the limits of our individual and collective success.

FOCUS #5: BEST PRACTICES FOR ONBOARDING NEW HIRES AND NEW STUDENTS

Once it was publicly known that Shackleton was putting together a crew for the Endurance, over 5,000 people (including men and women) applied for the privilege of being aboard. He would only need between

25 and 30 capable people; therefore, one of Shackleton's most pressing challenges early on was filtering out the thrill and glory seekers so that he could clearly see the team he needed. His process, though unorthodox, rarely failed. This is how he built his team. First, he needed a core group of veteran Antarctic seamen that he knew and could fully trust. Then, from that inner circle, he identified what roles he would need to fill. For example, he would need a cook, a doctor, a surgeon, a meteorologist, and able seamen to conduct the grunt work of sailing, to name a few. To ensure that his second and third-tier group was going to gel with his first tier, Shackleton employed an unconventional approach to interviewing candidates.

While he had a stringent, non-negotiable set of interpersonal characteristics that were required for his top brass, it appears that when he filled the lesser positions, he was more concerned with personality and team chemistry than individual skill. For instance, Leonard Hussey, the man that Shackleton hired to be his meteorologist, had never been a meteorologist prior to being added to the roster. Shackleton's interview with Hussey lasted less than five minutes, and he proved to be incredibly capable of performing his duties once he applied himself to the task. For others, Shackleton wanted to know if they could sing and if they had a sense of humor. It may appear to be odd, but Shackleton understood more than most what they were about face. He was not simply filling roles with people who could do jobs. He was building a team that would need to be able to get along as friends if they were going to achieve their mission. Shackleton knew that tasks could be learned, but team chemistry and personality were a luxury that his time frame could not afford. This piece of the puzzle needed to be in place from the beginning. Shackleton prioritized relationships above all else, even above skill. In this section, the lessons of Shackleton's relational priority are applied to online educational hiring practices and onboarding new students.

Using Shackleton's odd but effective team-building approach, I'd like to suggest the following three-step process for those in charge of hiring the needed positions of an online educational team. These steps include 1) building the core team, 2) identifying versatile and flexible team members, and 3) prioritizing team chemistry over individual skills. Furthermore, lessons can also be gleaned and applied from these steps with regard to onboarding new students into our programs so that we may minimize any feelings of insecurity and anxiety that the learner may encounter.

STEP 1: BUILD THE CORE TEAM

Just as Christian Jacobsen, the maker, and supervisor of the building of the Endurance, refused to allow men on his team who had never been to the frozen seas, Shackleton knew that he needed a core team of individuals in his inner circle who were seasoned Antarctic adventurers. Therefore, the position of second-in-command was given to his dear friend, Frank Wild. In 1908-1909, Wild had been with Shackleton on their race to the South Pole, and his temperament was the exact opposite of Shackleton's. Wild was a loyal member of the team, a calming presence for the crew, and provided the perfect emotional balance to Shackleton's sometimes "explosive" behavior. A sailor by the name of Thomas Crean was offered the position of 2nd Officer. In 1901 and again in 1910, Crean accompanied Robert Scott to the South Pole. Crean was one of the strongest, most disciplined, and experienced Antarctic sailors on the planet. Those skills would prove to be invaluable in the months ahead.

While Crean was a tall Irishman and a veteran of the Royal Navy, Alfred Cheetham, the 3rd Officer, was tiny with a kindhearted disposition. Cheetham was the exact opposite of Crean in both appearance and temperament. Having traveled to the Antarctic on three separate journeys, including one with Shackleton and one with Robert Scott, Cheetham was the most experienced of all of Shackleton's team. Finally, two more experienced men were added to this fantastic nucleus of leaders: George Marston, the team's artist, and Thomas McLeod, an able seaman. Marston was known for being an unpredictable and moody person, while Mcleod would prove to possess a courageous and steady nature. For example, while on this expedition, Mcleod's 49th birthday was celebrated by asking him to pretend to be a penguin so the crew could lure a giant sea leopard into a trap. That night, because of McLeod's steely nerve, the crew celebrated his birthday by adding 1,000 lbs. of leopard meat to their stores. Again, Mcleod appears to be the polar opposite of the moody artist Marston in personality. All of the members of Shackleton's core team had been to the Antarctic at least once before, and all of them had been personally observed in action by Shackleton himself.

Leadership Application #1

When building your core-team, look for people who not only have the crucial experience needed for the job, but they've returned from their difficult experiences hungry for more.

All of Shackleton's core group had been on at least one or two trips to the Antarctic. They had personally seen with their own eyes the potential threats and hazards that part of the world can present. Yet, they could not wait to return! When building your team, look for people who have been through some struggles and have been knocked down a few times, yet they keep getting back up again and again. Shackleton's approach to building his inner circle was to find people who had faced adversity and risen to become even stronger as a result. There were zero theoretical rookies in his core group.

Leadership Application #2

When building your core-team, look for people with complementary personalities.

Shackleton's core team was not made up of people just like him or people who would simply say "yes" to his every idea without genuine consideration. They were not mindless robots who were incapable of respectful dissent. While all of his core group was unquestionably loyal to Shackleton, undoubtedly committed to the mission, and ready to attempt what many would consider impossible goals, none of his inner circle were without their own ideas and would gladly share them if they felt it necessary. Shackleton looked for people who had complementary personalities with the people who would work nearest each other. As the old saying goes, opposites attract.

STEP 2: IDENTIFY VERSATILE AND FLEXIBLE TEAM MEMBERS

If there was one thing that Shackleton did not want on his team, it was drama. Not having a healthy and stable temperament could potentially be lethal for the members of the expedition. Yet, Shackleton hired a capricious artist, George Marston, a man known for being melancholy one moment and jovial the next. Marston had a reputation for being pessimistic and lacking personal initiative. So why did Shackleton allow him on the team? More than that, why was he invited into the inner circle of Shackleton's most trusted leaders? This was the nucleus around which every other hire would be determined. Why?

Shackleton's choice appears to be inconsistent until one understands what made Marston's attitude bearable – what made him so special. He was not only one of the most seasoned Antarctic travelers on the team. He wasn't just a very gifted sketch artist and painter who greatly contributed to the overall storyline. Marston was a man of many talents, and he allowed himself to be used beyond his primary job description. He was also a gifted carpenter and cobbler who would gladly lend a hand to repair the ship, as well as the torn sole in a boot. Marston had a reputation for doing all of his work with excellence. He was industrious, creative, and, most of all, trustworthy and integrous. Though he may have been given to bouts with depression, he was a team player. When the Endurance was stranded, wedged between massive ice flows, and they were forced to entertain themselves, Marston would willingly jump in and take part in the play or sing a song. And when the team needed an extra driver for the dog sleds, Marston volunteered, even though he had no previous experience. [12] After applying himself to the task, Marston became quite skilled at driving dog teams and even made leather whips for the others.

Leadership Application #3

When building your team, look for people with
a humble, willing, and flexible attitude.

An example of things that Marston never said to Shackleton was, "Sorry, that is not in my job description. Sorry, that is not what I signed up for. I'm an artist, nothing more." Always remember, when building a team, you will need people who are open-minded, willing, flexible, and able to learn new on-the-job skills. There were times when Marston was emotionally unsteady and difficult to deal with, even unliked by the team, but he was a good man. He was a man of impeccable character, humility, and flexibility. That is what made him an indispensable member of Shackleton's inner circle. That is what made him worth it all.

STEP 3: PRIORITIZE TEAM CHEMISTRY OVER INDIVIDUAL SKILL

Just as every individual piece of wood in the Endurance was "fitted with the closest tolerance; every joint and every fitting cross-braced something else for the maximum strength," [13] so too was the team itself cross-braced for its highest possible strength. Shackleton knew that he needed a ship that was built for the burden of the most treacherous waters in the world, and his crew could be no different. Just as the builders of the boat meticulously chose each plank, Shackleton was purposeful in the choices of each man. It is said of Shackleton that he could gain "easy rapport with men of all stripes." [14] To recruit this diverse team of men, some of whom had never performed the duties for which they were hired, an advertisement went out that is said to have read, "Men wanted for hazardous journey. Small wages, bitter cold, long months of complete darkness, constant danger, safe return doubtful. Honor and recognition in case of success." Though there are no remaining prints of this newspaper advertisement in existence today, it well represents the heart of Shackleton's call. As the leader, he wasn't looking for the best of the best individuals; he was looking for the right team.

Perhaps Shackleton learned this in his early days of Antarctic exploration when he met who was then the president of the Royal Geographical Society, Sir Clements Markham, who was more than willing to build a team around inexperienced men. Markham believed "good breeding counted more than a man's practical experience." For better or for worse, when it came to filling the blank spaces on Shackleton's roster, he prioritized team chemistry over individual skill.

For example, there is little doubt that more accomplished meteorologists applied to be on the team, but Shackleton hired Leonard Hussy due to his strong personality and unmistakable determination. Hussy was an experienced explorer, yes, but to the far reaches of the Sudan. One could not imagine a terrain that was more different from the Antarctic, but after just a few moments of meeting Hussy, Shackleton liked him and knew that he would fit.

Leadership Application #4

When building your team, look for people who have *both* an obvious social fit on the team coupled with a capacity to learn and grow into their role on the team.

Personality and overall team chemistry were prioritized over personal/individual talent or skill. Relational intelligence was just as important, if not more important, to Shackleton than mental acuity. This point is not to diminish the need to acquire the requisite skills, knowledge, and education for a position. However, when the position being filled involves working with others on a regular, daily, and consistent basis, interpersonal skills become a priority.

The study's findings and the literature review call the reader's attention to the need for improving onboarding and orientation practices for school employees and new students. In the literature review, data reveals the need to address the effects of social isolation through robust forms of professional training for all involved in online education and onboarding new students. [15] Additionally, when the needed preparation and onboarding strategies align with safe and trustworthy opportunities to interact, one's intellectual development grows. [16] The findings of the study concur. As Participant 14 stated, "I would have liked an onboarding/orientation class to help feel more confident and less isolated." Participant 14's greatest sense of social isolation came at the beginning of the semester. Therefore, the empirical implication within the study is that social isolation can be mitigated for the leaders and the learners before it becomes an issue should the correct resources and onboarding processes be offered before the class begins.

While the Endurance did not survive the journey, the team did – all 27 of them miraculously survived because of the attentive prework of their onboarding process. As a result of the study, it is recommended to all policymakers, leaders, and practitioners of online educational pathways to thoughtfully consider how they are building their teams with relationships at the top of the list of priorities. When relationships thrive and have an opportunity to grow and flourish, all benefit.

DISCUSS & JOURNAL

DISCUSSION QUESTIONS

For this journal entry, write and reflect on two of the leadership applications listed in this chapter. Then, discuss your journal entry with your team or classmates.

JOURNAL

_____

_____

_____

_____

_____

_____

_____

_____

_____

_____

_____

_____

_____

_____

_____

_____

CHAPTER 7
COMPONENTS OF CHRISTIAN ONLINE HIGHER EDUCATION

While most readers will be very familiar with the great hymn "Amazing Grace", it is less likely as many people will understand the meaning of the song through the lens of its author, John Newton. Newton's storied and somewhat unfathomable life offers particular significance to a *remotely close* classroom. After a near-death experience at sea, Newton was converted in a frantic appeal to God to save his life, and thus, his faith journey began. Though God had rescued his life and the lives of those on board the ship, Newton's faith was only just beginning. The long sanctifying work of the Holy Spirit, coupled with a renewal of his mind by washing it with the Word of God, was still very much required in the life of this new believer. When one zooms out to get the overall perspective of how abhorrently evil John Newton was before his conversion, it offers a fresh understanding of the "saved a wretch like me" line from his most famous hymn.

To say that John Newton was a despicable and grotesque sinner would be putting it mildly. In Newton's own words, he was "exceedingly vile and not only sinned with a high hand, but made it [his] study to tempt and seduce others upon every occasion." [1] Rebel, pervert, deserter, profane, blasphemer, drunkard, drug dealer, witchcraft, black magic, voodoo, lustful, rape, suicidal, depressed, and slave ship captain are all titles that Newton would have proudly and gladly worn prior to coming to Christ. Yet, even after he repented, many spiritual blindsides needed to be addressed. These blinders eventually faded, but only after Newton entered a Christian community of mentors and friends. Thus, the application and relevance of Newton's story to the *remotely close* classroom. The amazing account of God's grace in Newton's life highlights the transformational power of a Christian community – something that must be present in Christian online educational delivery systems.

As we approach the conclusion of this book, I'd like to revisit a few pivotal questions from its beginning. What sets Christian online education apart? In other words, how would you know Christian online education when you saw it? What Biblical paradigms of learning can be applied to our online pathways? Is it more Scripturally accurate to learn in isolation or a community? To what Biblical precedence can one look for guidance relating to the design of a learning delivery system? These are the questions that ultimately provoked this study, and it is the answers to these questions that I'd like to draw your attention to in the following sections.

When he was ten, John Newton stopped going to school and immediately went into the workforce to help his family. His education regarding the things of God had stopped sooner than that at the age of six. Though he had no extensive formal education, that does not mean that Newton was not very intelligent. After he was converted to Christianity, prayer and studying the Bible became his priority. As Newton put it, "My leisure time was chiefly employed in reading and meditating on the Scriptures and praying to the Lord for mercy and instruction." [2]

Not long after his fateful conversion day upon the rough and tumbled seas, Newton began to sense that God may want him to become a vocational minister within the Church of England, but that would require something that he did not have – formal education from the "right" schools and high proficiency in the Biblical languages of Latin, Hebrew, and Greek. From a natural point of view, the educational obstacles standing between Newton and ordination within the church were simply insurmountable. After all, there was no such thing as correspondence education in those days, and it was all but unheard of for someone of John Newton's age and history to transform himself into something desirable and useful for the church. Newton needed a miracle.

That said, "By dint of hard industry, often waking when I might have slept, I made some progress, I not only understood the sense and meaning of many odes and some of the epistles, but began to relish the beauties of the composition." [3] Upon his long and solitary days at sea, Newton interned himself in his quarters and became the prototypical self-taught, isolated learner. He committed hours upon hours daily with his dictionaries, lexicons, commentaries, and Bible. Eventually, due to Newton's persistence, he taught himself how to read, understand, and even translate Biblical languages far better than the average scholar from Oxford or Cambridge. It appears that with enough grit, hard work, and determination, a self-taught, isolated learner can rise above their present challenges. Yet, even with all of this newfound skill, knowledge, and understanding, there was something still amiss in Newton's heart.

At the beginning of this book, I mentioned that it is not my goal to argue against online learning and for in-person education, and I'll reiterate this point now. My aim in this book is not to condemn those who have learned alone, and praise those who learned in community. Furthermore, it is not my hope to somehow insinuate that a person cannot learn tremendous amounts of good information and gain helpful knowledge while learning alone. Additionally, this book does not purport that learning alone is sinful. Rather, I deeply desire to provide insight into the value and remarkable benefit of processing information within the context of a caring Christian community so that the information becomes transformational in one's life. The research findings indicate that it is possible for people to become educated in isolation; however, the overall long-term and short-term benefits of learning in a Christian community provide an unquestionably better experience for the student. Some participants even went as far as to say that learning in isolation left them feeling as though they were robbed of something special. That special something is the relational component of learning. After more than ten years of online education, earning my

Masters and Ph.D. in total isolation with no required in-person cohorts, zoom calls, or online office hours, I concur and empathize with the feeling of having been robbed. I admit that it was my choice to enroll in such a program, but at the end of it all, I can honestly say that I did not realize what I was missing until it was too late.

From 1749 to 1754, while aboard various ships, John Newton essentially taught himself how to read and translate Biblical languages on an incredibly high level of scholarship. Take a moment to pause and consider what this truly amazing scholastic achievement is. For a minimum of 3 hours every day in nearly complete solitude, Newton took care to ensure his devotional life of prayer and study took priority. However, even with all this effort, Newton felt something was amiss; study alone was simply "not enough." [4] What was missing? Christian community and fellowship with like-minded believers did not become a reality in Newton's life until May 1754. It was at this time that a man by the name of Captain Alexander Clunie entered John's world and forever changed it. Clunie was the first of many spiritual mentors who helped Newton ground his vast knowledge of the Word of God in the deep soils of the Christian Gospel. This was the time when Newton's head-knowledge morphed into a brand-new heart. More names were quickly added to the list of what Newton called his "spiritual friends." [5] Some of them went on to become trendsetters of global gospel movements. Men like "Samuel Brewer, George Whitefield, Henry Crooke, Henry Venn, William Grimshaw, and John Wesley helped Newton's faith to become earthed and securely rooted in the gospel." [6] Did Newton attain incredibly high levels of knowledge while in total isolation? Absolutely. However, that information did not become transformational until he could process that information within the context of a caring Christian community. As Newton said, "It is difficult to come to faith on one's own without good teachers." [7]

Newton's story offers us a wonderful example of what the book is attempting to prove, and that is simply this: relationships matter when it comes to one's education. A mentor and spiritual friend of mine used to say to me regarding people like John Newton, "His house was built, but the light was not yet on." The strong structure of

Newton's theological prowess had been built, but the lights of salvation, inspiration, and transformation did not shine in his heart until Godly mentors and teachers became a regular part of his life.

Space would not permit me to do an exhaustive and systematic theology of learning communities within Scripture, but I would like to highlight a few that have spoken to me over the years. Even the casual reading of the Old and New Testaments would quickly reveal community. It is illustrated in the Holy Trinity and Heavenly council (Gen. 1:26; Isaiah 6:8), the family unit (Gen. 18; Deut. 6:7; Deut. 11:19; Prov. 22:6), the Levitical/Priestly system (Lev. 10; 2 Chr. 35:3; Ezra 7:6; Neh. 8), the Prophets (1 Sam. 12:20-23), the School/Sons of the Prophets (1 Sam. 10 & 19; 1 Kings 20; 2 Kings 2 & 4), the Kings (2 Chr. 17; 1 Kings 10) and the Rabbinical systems of the New Testament (Matthew 23; Mark 1:22; Luke 2:46-52). A cursory study of the text would offer the learner enough evidence to believe that God's normative plan for learning and leadership development is that of community learning. I acknowledge the presence of outliers in the Bible that do not fit within the typical educational boxes. However, overall, the idea of a lone-ranger leader/learner is simply absent in the Scripture. Furthermore, one would be extremely hard-pressed to find a Scriptural recommendation for long-term learning and leadership development that takes place exclusively in isolation.

There are three examples within the Biblical text that I believe illustrate the point beautifully, and it is to their stories that I now draw your attention.

EZRA & THE LEVITES (NEHEMIAH 8:4-8 ESV)

4 And Ezra the scribe stood on a wooden platform that they had made for the purpose. And beside him stood Mattithiah, Shema, Anaiah, Uriah, Hilkiah, and Maaseiah on his right hand, and Pedaiah, Mishael, Malchijah, Hashum, Hashbaddanah, Zechariah, and Meshullam on his left hand. 5 And Ezra opened the book in the sight of all the people, for he was above all the people, and as he opened it all the people stood. 6 And Ezra blessed the Lord, the great God, and all the people answered, "Amen, Amen," lifting up their hands. And they bowed their heads and worshiped the Lord with their faces to the ground. 7 Also Jeshua, Bani, Sherebiah, Jamin, Akkub, Shabbethai, Hodiah, Maaseiah, Kelita, Azariah, Jozabad, Hanan, Pelaiah, the Levites, helped the people to understand the Law, while the people remained in their places. 8 They read from the book, from the Law of God, clearly, and they gave the sense, so that the people understood the reading.

Notice immediately that the speaker/teacher is not alone on the platform. Ezra has at least 13 assistants. Nothing about this moment is hidden, isolated, or secretive. The leaders are in front of all the people, and the book is opened in the sight of all the people. This is community learning at its finest. This powerful spiritual support system results in collective prayer, blessings, worship, and humble repentance. A personal, emotional, and spiritual connection between the leaders and the learners is apparent as the presence of God descends. Then, a group of a minimum of 13 Levites took the people into what amounts to breakout sessions to allow this large crowd to process the information they had just heard in a caring community. In these small groups, the Levites explained the lesson clearly, and they gave the sense so that the people understood the reading. After a very long spiritual dry spell, the people of Israel were hungry for truth, but they were incredibly ignorant of what God had commanded them to do. There had been a breakdown of various community structures and a loss of access to the Word of the Lord. To remedy these problems, learning and processing information in the context of a community of caring and like-minded believers was the answer.

THE ETHIOPIAN EUNUCH (ACTS 8: 26-31 ESV)

26 Now an angel of the Lord said to Philip, "Rise and go toward the south to the road that goes down from Jerusalem to Gaza." This is a desert place. 27 And he rose and went. And there was an Ethiopian, a eunuch, a court official of Candace, queen of the Ethiopians, who was in charge of all her treasure. He had come to Jerusalem to worship 28 and was returning, seated in his chariot, and he was reading the prophet Isaiah. 29 And the Spirit said to Philip, "Go over and join this chariot." 30 So Philip ran to him and heard him reading Isaiah the prophet and asked, "Do you understand what you are reading?" 31 And he said, "How can I, unless someone guides me?" And he invited Philip to come up and sit with him.

The first time Scripture records God's displeasure was in Genesis 2:18-25 when God said that it was not good for man to be alone. In Acts 8, it appears that the Holy Spirit is just as concerned for the soul of this lone learner, the Ethiopian Eunuch. The Queen's court official was traveling along the desert road and reading from the scroll of Isaiah without any way of gaining an understanding. Both his physical location and his spiritual circumstance reflect isolation. Does this person have access to good information? Yes, he does. Would it be possible for him to learn something that he did not know before after he finished reading? Yes, it is. But would he come to a saving knowledge of Jesus Christ and arrive at the text's true meaning without a teacher? Apparently not. Philip asks, "Do you understand what you are reading?" The court official responded, "How can I, unless someone guides me?" The end result of learning and processing with someone who knows more is truly transformational. Look at what it says in verses 35-38.

35 Then Philip opened his mouth, and beginning with this Scripture, he told him the good news about Jesus. 36 And as they were going along the road, they came to some water, and the eunuch said, "See, here is water! What prevents me from being baptized?" 38 And he commanded the chariot to stop, and they both went down into the water, Philip and the eunuch, and he baptized him.

It was not good for Adam to be alone in the eyes of the Lord, so he made him a helper named Eve. Neither was it good for the Ethiopian Eunuch to be alone as he did his best to learn from a desert place, so God sent him a helper named Philip. The end result was lasting and eternal change.

APOLLOS (ACTS 18:24-28 ESV)

24 Now a Jew named Apollos, a native of Alexandria, came to Ephesus. He was an eloquent man, competent in the Scriptures. 25 He had been instructed in the way of the Lord. And being fervent in spirit, he spoke and taught accurately the things concerning Jesus, though he knew only the baptism of John. 26 He began to speak boldly in the synagogue, but when Priscilla and Aquila heard him, they took him aside and explained to him the way of God more accurately. 27 And when he wished to cross to Achaia, the brothers encouraged him and wrote to the disciples to welcome him. When he arrived, he greatly helped those who through grace had believed, 28 for he powerfully refuted the Jews in public, showing by the Scriptures that the Christ was Jesus.

Alexandria was the second largest city in the entire empire of Rome. It was equipped with one of the world's largest libraries and was home to every available educational resource known to man. No doubt Apollos was a beneficiary of these local treasures and became highly effective in communicating God's Word, including public debate. Growing up in a culture that valued literature, education, history, philosophy, public discourse, and debate, Apollos learned from some of the best the skills necessary to captivate an audience. Though we do not know the entire salvation testimony of Apollos, we do know that he was,

1. instructed correctly in the way of Jesus,
2. passionate in spirit as he spoke and taught about Jesus,
3. was accurate in what he taught concerning the Lord,
4. was bold and unafraid to oppose in public those who wished to discredit Jesus or his followers, and
5. he still had more to learn.

Verse 26 tells us that there were two disciples of Paul the Apostle in attendance that day, and "when Priscilla and Aquila heard him, they took him aside and explained to him the way of God more accurately." I do not know exactly what they said to Apollos, but this much is clear. Though highly educated and effective in his ministry, he still had more to learn. To go to the next level, Apollos needed to process some information in the context of a loving Christian community. While I do not know what Priscilla and Aquila told him after they took him aside, I do know that it helped him to become even more effective in what God had called him to do. Did Apollos know some very good things accurately before meeting Priscilla and Aquila? Absolutely! Did Apollos have more to learn? Was there yet another level to which he needed to rise? Yes! Yes! Yes! Learning and processing information with those who love and support you and who long to impart next-level learning into your life is simply irreplaceable.

There are countless examples in the Bible that would play out in similar form, but the point has been made – to grow to the highest levels of learning, the normative Biblical paradigm is to do so within a community of like-minded and knowledgeable believers. The value of a learning community cannot be overstated, and it appears to be the Scriptural precedence for which we are called to reach. Doing so takes all involved to new levels of effective leadership and professional development. This point is clearly illustrated by the accounts of Biblical leaders, as well as the incredible stories of those like John Newton. The *lone-ranger* learner or leader simply does not have the capacity to rise to their highest potential apart from the Biblical design of a learning community.

DISCUSS & JOURNAL

DISCUSSION QUESTIONS

For this journal entry, reflect upon why you agree with or disagree with the theological arguments that have been made in this chapter. Can you think of any outliers in the Bible that appear to have been totally formed in isolation by the Lord for their calling? Then discuss your answers in your team or with your classmates.

JOURNAL

_____

_____

_____

_____

_____

_____

_____

_____

_____

_____

_____

_____

_____

_____

_____

CONCLUSION

"You will never go to college, and neither will your children." As my father struggled in his grade school subjects sitting in a one-room school house with children of all ages, this alleged teacher pronounced these destructive words over his impressionable heart. What made her believe it was okay to say such things to a child? It is unimaginable to me. This declaration hovered over my father's ambitions like a concrete ceiling for years. If she had the temerity to say it to him, how many other children did those exact words scar over the years? How many of her pupils lived out their days believing this vicious lie, unable to rise above it? The words of a teacher have the power to reach into a person's future. Their words have the power to give life and hope or death and despair.

Some of my earliest memories include moving from our home in Tennessee to Broken Arrow, Oklahoma, where my father had enrolled in a Bible School. It was the early 1980s, and he sensed that the Lord wanted him to prepare for vocational ministry. Like any student who steps out in faith to further their education, obstacles quickly emerge. At this point, my dad was married with two young children. How could he afford to go to school? How would he have time to work enough hours to provide for his family and still attend class? Question after heavy question bubbled to the forefront. Even before we could unload the first box from our moving truck, my father saw how much more the cost of living was to be, and he seriously considered turning around in retreat before he even started. Yet, God's call remained, and the still, small, reassuring voice of the Spirit enabled him to unpack each box by faith. Somehow, it all worked. A few years later, my father graduated, and we moved back home to Tennessee to see what was next on God's list of to-dos. The stranglehold of the curse of the one room school house teacher was beginning to loosen. Her lies were beginning to bow down to the truth of God's Word, but that is not the end of the story.

Look again at the teacher's obscenity: "You will never go to college, and *neither will your children*." She was passing a belief system onto my father and his *future*. The fantastic thing about this story is that my older brother and I never heard about it until *after* we had earned a college degree. Not once in my entire life did my father pass on the foreboding weight of his former "teacher." The curse of his past had been broken. My brother went on to graduate from college, as did I, but my father's inspirational story was still not finished. God had more in store for him.

At the age of 65, when many are contemplating which golf cart to purchase and which retirement village best suits their needs, my father was retreading his spiritual tires. The Holy Spirit again whispered into his heart, "Start over." God was calling my father to start over and begin again from a place of lifelong experience. It had been more than 25 years since he had taken a class; the same old questions that haunted him back in the early 80's resurfaced. How would he afford it? Where would he find the time? Etc. Etc. Etc. If he needed an excuse not to obey the Lord, he could have easily found one. But no excuse would stand in his way.

When the first box of books arrived in the mail, my father became so overwhelmed with fear and anxiety that he literally closed the box and sent it back. But as the old saying goes, "If it is God's will, it is God's bill. Where he guides, he provides." And provide the Lord did – in big ways! At 65, my father moved forward in faith, enrolled in an online program, earned a Bachelor of Science, and seamlessly entered his M.Div. program. After years of perseverance, the Lord gave my father a birthday present he'd never forget. On December 16, 2017, my father officially turned in his final assignment and earned a Master of Divinity on his 70th birthday – and it was all accomplished *online!*

If it were not for this remote educational solution, finding a way to "start over" would have been even more difficult. Online education was the tool the Lord provided to answer the questions of how and when. Due to technological advancements in learning delivery systems, my father overcame the foul words that spewed from the one-room school house of his past. Currently, my dad is an online adjunct professor, paying it forward to the next generation.

As we come to the close, allow me to encourage you to rise above the voices of discouragement and fear. Take a moment to listen to the sayings that my brother and I heard on a near-daily basis from my parents. Words that I now speak over the lives of my children.

If God is for you (and He most definitely is), no one can stand against you. You are more than a conqueror in Christ Jesus! You can do all things through Christ who strengthens you. God has not given you a spirit of fear but of power, love, and a sound mind! If Christ Jesus lives in you, the ONE in you is greater than the one in the World! You are the head and not the tail. Blessed going and coming. Blessed in the city and the country. Above and not beneath.

Those were the words that my brother and I heard regularly. My father and mother protected us from the ill words of their past and instead gave us the promises of God! These are the words that my wife and I now tell our children.

These promises carried me across the finish line of a doctoral degree, and countless other challenges over the years. These same promises are yours in Jesus' Name! Stand on the fact that these promises will take you where God has called you to go as well.

DISCUSS & JOURNAL

DISCUSSION

In this journal entry, reflect on the following questions and discuss them in a group if you feel comfortable doing so.

- What "words of the past" have you had to personally overcome?
- Do you struggle with negative self-talk? What does that look like for you and what circumstances typically trigger the negative thought patterns?
- Do you have a group of people in your life that build you up and continue to encourage you with the Word of God?

JOURNAL

_____

_____

_____

_____

_____

_____

_____

_____

_____

_____

_____

NOW WHAT?

Afterword by: Dr. Earl Creps

I departed Christian Higher Education for church planting at the dawn of online coursework. My own ministry training had been conventional in the extreme, starting with correspondence courses that required us to mail in our assignments. Eventually, this "pony express" system gave way to a distance classroom experience using travel to make my MA possible. These systems all had a common feature: paper. A paper syllabus required me to read paper books and compose hard copy assignments. The idea of raising up leaders in any other way seemed absurd or even harmful, because we would not be in the same room together, a vital requirement of discipleship as we understood it.

Then, just before my departure for church planting, the seminary where I served (the Assemblies of God Theological Seminary) asked me to design their first online course. At that point, I had heard of these, but had never actually seen one. But neither had almost anyone else I knew. So, with no training and even less experience, I started chiseling an "online" class from the mass of materials I had developed for in-person courses.

In other words, I amalgamated my existing lecture notes, Power Point slides, videos, and reading assignments on the subject, called that a syllabus, and then trusted our tech people to make it all appear on the internet for students to access. And a few of them did. What they encountered online was little more than my face-to-face class presented on a screen—an electronic pony express.

Our goal was to create greater access to seminary courses for those who could not reach our physical location. And this remains the primary goal today: *expanded access*. Countless students, me included, have benefited from online education that did not require them to quit their jobs, sell their homes, and move to the provider's site. Instead, the provider now brings access to us. But the question remains, *access to what?*

I returned to higher education about ten years later to find a new world. Everything had changed. Education on the college level was now dominated by online models, with Christian ministry training catching up rapidly. I had missed it all.

Ironically, my new job at Northwest University would be founding and directing a hybrid PhD/EdD program that used online courses extensively. The training and development work with our team became a rigorous online education boot camp. I was trained on two different platforms as both an internet course designer and an instructor.

And then the Pandemic hit. Our on-campus classes were dispersed rapidly into online versions. My wife and I both taught a group of undergraduates in one of these. I never saw a better example of how bringing people together online can bypass their humanity in unforeseen ways. In other words, *access alone is not enough*. As our Zoom sessions started, some students stayed in bed with their blankets covering their heads. Others seemed to be almost frozen in place. The fear was almost palpable, with our discussions of course issues sometimes seeming contrived and pointless. Once again, the question was access to what? People in shock care little about the content or the convenience of our classes.

This is the point at which Dr. Day's notion of "remotely close" is a help. He points out that the internet and its delivery systems are useful technologies but they are *not magic.* For example, even the excellent training I received did little to address the need of our students to feel connected. The pandemic being the elephant in the room, they saw little reason to spend an hour online discussing the world's more generic problems when one positive test result could prove to be a death sentence.

I'll always be grateful to that quiet group of distracted freshmen. They helped me realize that I was designing and teaching online courses in a vacuum. They highlighted the difference between seeing each other's faces on a laptop screen, and feeling a connection that forms personal, spiritual, and academic bonds.

What Dr. Day's work helps us to understand is that, just being present on screen is not enough. The entire team responsible for mounting classrooms online must have a heart-level commitment to bonding students and faculty into a learning community. No matter what the technology, this project is a fundamentally human and spiritual enterprise.

That priority must then be embodied in both teaching methods and curricular design and student relationships until being "remotely close" is simply the default posture of the course. Without this dimension, we've developed only a fancier pony express.

Collectively, these factors are more an issue of each course's *culture* than its *syllabus*. And that's the exciting thing: in addition to its formal elements, every course can be a small (or large) "pop up" community in which professors are both leaders and instructors. When it works, it's a great job. When it doesn't, we are serving below our potential. As Pittsburgh Steeler football coach Chuck Knoll famously said, "When you're losing, everything they say about you is true."

Dr. Day's work inspires me to strive for this sort of connective culture. I am excited to continue the work of teaching online with the goal of forming communities in which we don't just study, but we are transformed together. To accomplish this objective, we can no longer just teach, as important as that is. We must lead.

APPENDIX 1

Participant 1

Interviewee 1 holds a Doctorate, served as a seminary president for more than fifteen years, was on the teaching faculty for another university for more than twenty years, and has been employed as an administrator/faculty member of three distinct schools of higher learning. Interviewee 1 has six years of online teaching experience and six years of online classroom design experience.

Participant 2

Interviewee 2 served as a founding director/dean of the Leadership Ph.D. and Ed.D. program at a university. Interviewee 2 has six years of online teaching experience five years of online classroom design experience, and has been employed by five unique schools of higher learning. Interviewee 2 has earned a Ph.D. and a Doctorate of Ministry.

Participant 3

Interviewee 3 has been teaching online for more than four years, has four years of online classroom design experience, and has worked for six different schools of higher education. Interviewee 3 earned a Master of Divinity and a Doctorate of Ministry.

Participant 4

Interviewee 4 earned a Master's degree, has thirteen years of online teaching experience at a college, has thirteen years of experience with online classroom design, and has been employed by one university.

Interviewee 4 is a co-founder of an online school of ministry and leadership.

Participant 5

Interviewee 5 earned a Doctorate in education, has five years of online teaching experience, three years of online classroom design experience, and has been employed by one university. Interviewee 5 is a co-founder of an online school of ministry and leadership.

Participant 6

Interviewee 6 holds a Doctorate of education and has eight years of online teaching experience, eight years of experience as an online student, designed two online courses, and has been employed by one university. Interviewee 6 brings years of administrative and educational experience to this study and has been the director of several educational initiatives.

Participant 7

Interviewee 7 has a Doctorate of Ministry degree, thirteen years of online teaching experience, thirteen years of online classroom design experience, and has been employed at three separate colleges. For more than a decade, Interviewee 7 was an administrator and a dean at a university.

Participant 8

Interviewee 8 has a Doctorate, four years of online teaching experience, two years of online classroom design, six years of experience as an online student, and has been employed at two different schools of higher learning. Furthermore, Interviewee 8 brings years of educational administrative experience to this study.

Participant 9

Interviewee 9 has a Doctorate, twelve years of online teaching experience, four years of experience as an online student, eight years of experience in online classroom design, and has been employed at one university. Interviewee 9 directs a business and leadership program at a university.

Participant 10

Interviewee 10 holds a Doctorate, has nineteen years of online teaching experience, twelve years of online classroom design experience, and has been employed by one school of higher education. Interviewee 10 is a department chair at a university.

Participant 11

Interviewee 11 has earned two degrees from two separate universities and holds a Doctorate of Ministry. Interviewee 11 has been the President of a seminary, has held multiple other administrative/ VP roles in other schools of higher learning, and has been employed by two universities. Interviewee 11 has twelve years of experience in online teaching and twelve years of experience in online classroom design.

Participant 12

Interviewee 12 will soon have a doctorate. In addition to the forthcoming doctorate, Interviewee 12 holds two Master's Degrees and a Bachelor's Degree. Interviewee 12 comes to this study with twelve years of experience in online teaching, five years of experience in online classroom design, and multiple years of administrative experience at a university. Interviewee 12 has been employed by one university for nearly twenty years.

Participant 13

Interviewee 13 has an earned Doctorate and more than 25 years of educational experience, which includes being a college president, vice president, registrar, and faculty member. Interviewee 13 has sixteen years of experience as an online teacher, four years of experience with online classroom design, and has been employed at two colleges.

Participant 14

Interviewee 14 is an online college student. Interviewee 14 has two years of online education experience with twelve credits earned towards a degree.

Participant 15

Interviewee 15 is an online college student with one and a half years of online educational experience and nine credits earned thus far.

Participant 16

Interviewee 16 comes to this study with seven years of online educational experience and one hundred thirty-five credit hours earned at university. Interviewee 16 has earned a Master's degree and a Doctoral degree.

Participant 17

Interviewee 17 comes to this study with five years of online educational experience and has earned a Master's Degree and a Doctorate of Ministry. Furthermore, Interviewee 17 has served as a doctoral chairperson and has recently been added to the adjunct faculty of a university.

APPENDIX 2

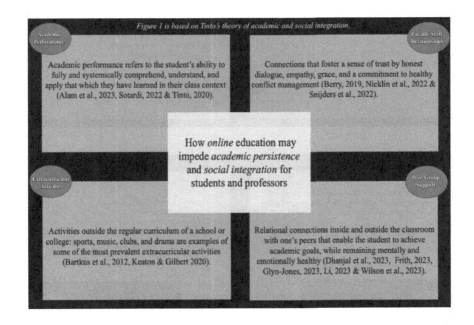

Figure 1 is based on Tinto's theory of academic and social integration.

Academic Performance

Academic performance refers to the student's ability to fully and systemically comprehend, understand, and apply that which they have learned in their class context (Alam et al., 2023, Sotardi, 2022 & Tinto, 2020).

Faculty/Staff Relationships

Connections that foster a sense of trust by honest dialogue, empathy, grace, and a commitment to healthy conflict management (Berry, 2019, Nicklin et al., 2022 & Snijders et al., 2022).

How *online* education may impede *academic persistence* and *social integration* for students and professors

Extracurricular Activities

Activities outside the regular curriculum of a school or college: sports, music, clubs, and drama are examples of some of the most prevalent extracurricular activities (Bartkus et al., 2012, Keaton & Gilbert 2020).

Peer-Group Support

Relational connections inside and outside the classroom with one's peers that enable the student to achieve academic goals, while remaining mentally and emotionally healthy (Dhanjal et al., 2023, Frith, 2023, Glyn-Jones, 2023, Li, 2023 & Wilson et al., 2023).

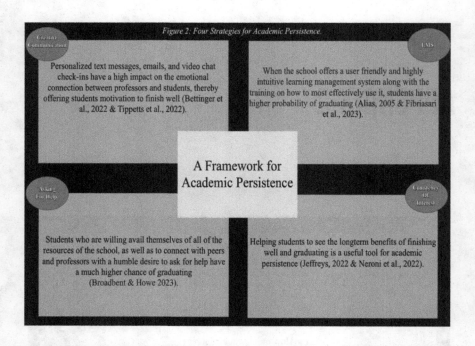

Figure 2: Four Strategies for Academic Persistence.

Creative Communication

Personalized text messages, emails, and video chat check-ins have a high impact on the emotional connection between professors and students, thereby offering students motivation to finish well (Bettinger et al., 2022 & Tippetts et al., 2022).

LMS

When the school offers a user friendly and highly intuitive learning management system along with the training on how to most effectively use it, students have a higher probability of graduating (Alias, 2005 & Fibriasari et al., 2023).

A Framework for Academic Persistence

Asking For Help.

Students who are willing avail themselves of all of the resources of the school, as well as to connect with peers and professors with a humble desire to ask for help have a much higher chance of graduating (Broadbent & Howe 2023).

Consistency Of Interest

Helping students to see the longterm benefits of finishing well and graduating is a useful tool for academic persistence (Jeffreys, 2022 & Neroni et al., 2022).

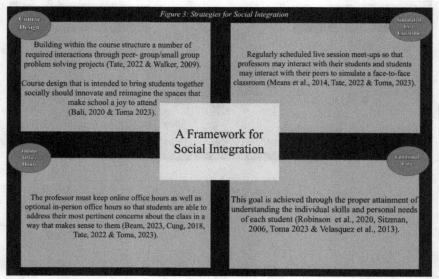

Figure 3: Strategies for Social Integration

Course Design

Building within the course structure a number of required interactions through peer- group/small group problem solving projects (Tate, 2022 & Walker, 2009).

Course design that is intended to bring students together socially should innovate and reimagine the spaces that make school a joy to attend (Bali, 2020 & Toma 2023).

Simulated Live Classtime

Regularly scheduled live session meet-ups so that professors may interact with their students and students may interact with their peers to simulate a face-to-face classroom (Means et al., 2014, Tate, 2022 & Toma, 2023).

A Framework for Social Integration

Online Office Hours

The professor must keep online office hours as well as optional in-person office hours so that students are able to address their most pertinent concerns about the class in a way that makes sense to them (Beam, 2023, Cung, 2018, Tate, 2022 & Toma, 2023).

Emotional Care

This goal is achieved through the proper attainment of understanding the individual skills and personal needs of each student (Robinson et al., 2020, Sitzman, 2006, Toma 2023 & Velasquez et al., 2013).

FIGURES 1 -3 DESIGNED BY DR. DANIEL DAY

APPENDIX 3

Table of Theoretical Implications	
Implication #1	Having a healthy learning community accentuated by social integration leads to successful educational outcomes and combats the effects of social isolation due to remote learning. (Lakhal et al., 2020 & Tinto, 1975, 1993, 2022).
Implication #2	Academic success is far less likely if a student does not connect beyond the classroom and socially integrate themselves into the full fellowship of the school (Lakhal et al., 2020 & Tinto, 2007).n
Implication #3	By giving students access to social supporters like peer mentors, counselors and coaches, the greater likelihood of academic success (Lakhal et al., 2020 & Tinto, 2007).
Implication #4	The theory explains that the level of involvement marks the student's social integration in extracurricular activities and the constant evidence of constructive relationships with the academic community (Baird, 2000 & Lakhal et al., 2020).
Implication #5	Students feel a sense of belonging when a healthy working and learning environment or learning community exists. Out of that sense of belongingness, students are inspired to develop and grow academically and personally (Tinto, 1975, 1993, 2022).
Implication #6	Healthy relationships are at the root of any solution proposed in this study, and Tinto would also infer closeness with one's peers and professors (Tinto, 1975, 1993, 2022).
Implication #7	According to Tinto, social integration is marked by an evident lack of social isolation on the part of the student (Liu, 2000 & Tinto, 1987).
Implication #8	For Tinto, academic integration happens when the learner shows a high level of intellectual growth and perceives their environment positively (Baird, 2000 & Lakhal et al., 2020).

APPENDIX 4

Table of Empirical Implications	
Implication #1	The quality of the teacher (Shin, 2021 & Kollalpitiya et al., 2020), the flexibility of one's schedule (Rath et al., 2019 & Van Wart et al., 2020), a sense that the educator is available, and present (Rath et al., 2019 & Van Wart et al., 2020)
Implication #2	The user-friendly application of the online platform (Rath et al., 2019; Shin, 2021 & Van Wart et al., 2020), access to quality computer equipment and internet (Abdullah, 2022; Harefa, 2022, & Pradana et al., 2021). Not all educators have been taught the skills or tools to create meaningful online communities (Ferri, 2020 & Morgan, 2022). (page 35)
Implication #3	Emotional and motivational support (Harefa, 2022 & Shin, 2021),
Implication #4	Timeliness in grading feedback (Sopina, 2015 & Watkins et al., 2014).
Implication #5	The ability to find and filter the information one needs to succeed academically largely depends on the training and onboarding process of the school (Abduraxmanova, 2022 & Lakhal et al., 2020).

CHAPTER 1 SOURCE MATERIAL

[1]   McCullough, D. (2005). 1776. Simon and Schuster.

[2]   Henry Knox. George Washington's Mount Vernon. (n.d.). https://www.mountvernon.org/library/digitalhistory/ digital-encyclopedia/article/henry-knox

[3]   McCullough, D. (2005). 1776. Simon and Schuster.

[4]   Henry Knox. George Washington's Mount Vernon. (n.d.). https://www.mountvernon.org/library/digitalhistory/ digital-encyclopedia/article/henry-knox

[5]   McCullough, D. (2005). 1776. Simon and Schuster.

[6]   Eun, B. (2019). The zone of proximal development as an overarching concept: A framework for synthesizing vygotsky's theories. *Educational Philosophy and Theory, 51*(1), 18 30. https:// doi.org/10.1080/00131857.2017.1421941

George, A., McEwan, A., & Tarr, J. (2021). Accountability in educational dialogue on attrition rates: Understanding external attrition factors and isolation in online law school. *Australasian Journal of Educational Technology, 37*(1), 111-132. https://doi.org/10.14742/ajet.6175

Hehir, E., Zeller, M., Luckhurst, J., & Chandler, T. (2021). Developing student connectedness under remote learning using digital resources: A systematic review. *Education and Information Technologies, 26*(5), 6531-6548. doi.org/10.1007/ s10639-021-10577-1

Leal Filho, W., Wall, T., Rayman-Bacchus, L., Mifsud, M., Pritchard, D. J., Lovren, V. O.,Farinha, C., Petrovic, D. S., & Balogun, A.-L. (2021). Impacts of covid-19 and social isolation on academic staff and students at universities: A cross-sectional study. *BMC Public Health, 21*(1). https://doi.org/10.1186/s12889-021-11040-z

Newman, S., & Latifi, A. (2021). Vygotsky, education, and teacher education. *Journal of Education for Teaching : JET, 47*(1), 4- 17. doi.org/10.1080/02607476.2020.1831375

[7]   Ferri, F., Grifoni, P., & Guzzo, T. (2020). Online learning and emergency remote teaching: Opportunities and challenges in emergency situations. *Societies (Basel, Switzerland), 10(4),* 86. https://doi.org/10.3390/soc10040086

Lambert, D., & Rosales, B. M. (2020). California school districts struggled to prepare teachers for distance learning this fall. *EdSource: Oakland, CA, USA.*

Scherer, R., Howard, S. K., Tondeur, J., & Siddiq, F. (2021). Profiling teachers' readiness for online teaching and learning in higher education: Who's ready? *Computers in Human Behavior, 118,* 106675. https://doi.org/10.1016/j.chb.2020.106675

[8]   Dong, Y., & Ishige, A. (2022). Studying abroad from home: An exploration of international graduate students' perceptions and experiences of emergency remote teaching. *Education Sciences, 12*(2), 98. https://doi.org/10.3390/educsci12020098

Mizani, H., Cahyadi, A., Hendryadi, H., Salamah, S., & Retno Sari, S. (2022). Loneliness, student engagement, and academic achievement during emergency remote teaching during COVID-19: The role of the god locus of control. *Humanities & Social Sciences Communications, 9*(1), 305- 305. https://doi.org/10.1057/s41599-022-01328-9

Morgan, H. (2022). Alleviating the challenges with remote learning during a pandemic. *Education Sciences, 12*(2), 109. https://doi.org/10.3390/educsci12020109

[9]   Cudjoe, T. K. M., & Kotwal, A. A. (2020). "Social distancing" amid a crisis in social isolation and loneliness. *Journal of the American*

Geriatrics Society (JAGS), 68(6), E27-E29. https://doi.org/10.1111/jgs.16527

Leal Filho, W., Wall, T., Rayman-Bacchus, L., Mifsud, M., Pritchard, D. J., Lovren, V. O.,Farinha, C., Petrovic, D. S., & Balogun, A.-L. (2021). Impacts of covid-19 and social isolation on academic staff and students at universities: A cross-sectional study. *BMC Public Health*, *21*(1). https://doi.org/10.1186/s12889-021-11040-z

[10]   Dong, Y., & Ishige, A. (2022). Studying abroad from home: An exploration of international graduate students' perceptions and experiences of emergency remote teaching. *Education Sciences*, *12*(2), 98. https://doi.org/10.3390/educsci12020098

Mizani, H., Cahyadi, A., Hendryadi, H., Salamah, S., & Retno Sari, S. (2022). Loneliness, student engagement, and academic achievement during emergency remote teaching during COVID-19: The role of the god locus of control. *Humanities & Social Sciences Communications*, *9*(1), 305- 305. https://doi.org/10.1057/s41599-022-01328-9

Morgan, H. (2022). Alleviating the challenges with remote learning during a pandemic. *Education Sciences*, *12*(2), 109. https://doi.org/10.3390/educsci12020109

[11]   Morese, R. (2020). Social isolation: An interdisciplinary view. Intech Open.

[12]   Eriksen, E. V., & Bru, E. (2023). Investigating the links of social-emotional competencies: emotional well-being and academic engagement among adolescents. *Scandinavian Journal of Educational Research*, *67*(3), 391-405.

Skinner, E. A., Kindermann, T. A., & Furrer, C. J. (2009). A motivational perspective on engagement and disaffection: Conceptualization and assessment of children's behavioral and emotional participation in academic activities in the classroom. *Educational and psychological measurement*, *69*(3), 493-525.

[13]   Alam, F., Lim, Y. C., Chaw, L. L., Idris, F., & Kok, K. Y. Y. (2023). Multiple mini- interviews is a predictor of students' academic achievements in early undergraduate medical years: A retrospective study. *BMC Medical Education, 23*(1), 187-187. https://doi.org/10.1186/s12909-023-04183-7

Sotardi, V. A. (2022). On institutional belongingness and academic performance: Mediating effects of social self-efficacy and metacognitive strategies. *Studies in Higher Education, 47*(12), 2444–2459. https://doi.org/10.1080/03075079.2022.2081678

Tinto, V. (2020). "Learning Better Together." In *Transitioning Students Into Higher Education: Philosophy, Pedagogy, and Practice*, edited by A. Olds, 13–24. Routledge.

[14]   Alcuetas, E. S. (2019). Becoming a better version of me: A study on the resiliency of reunified young adult Filipino immigrants in Norway (Master's thesis, University of Stavanger, Norway).

Allan, J. F., & McKenna, J. (2019). Outdoor adventure builds resilient learners for higher education: A quantitative analysis of the active components of positive change. *Sports, 7*(5), 122.

Howard, S. & Johnson, B. (2000). What makes the difference? Children and teachers talk about resilient outcomes for children 'at risk'. *Educational Studies, 26*, 321-337.

Martin, A. (2002). Motivation and academic resilience: Developing a model for student enhancement. *Australian journal of education, 46*(1), 34-49.

[15]   Alcuetas, E. S. (2019). Becoming a better version of me: A study on the resiliency of reunified young adult Filipino immigrants in Norway (Master's thesis, University of Stavanger, Norway).

Allan, J. F., & McKenna, J. (2019). Outdoor adventure builds resilient learners for higher education: A quantitative analysis of the active components of positive change. *Sports, 7*(5), 122.

Howard, S. & Johnson, B. (2000). What makes the difference? Children and teachers talk about resilient outcomes for children 'at risk'. *Educational Studies, 26*, 321-337.

Martin, A. (2002). Motivation and academic resilience: Developing a model for student enhancement. *Australian journal of education, 46*(1), 34-49.

[16] Alcuetas, E. S. (2019). Becoming a better version of me: A study on the resiliency of reunified young adult Filipino immigrants in Norway (Master's thesis, University of Stavanger, Norway).

Allan, J. F., & McKenna, J. (2019). Outdoor adventure builds resilient learners for higher education: A quantitative analysis of the active components of positive change. *Sports, 7*(5), 122.

Howard, S. & Johnson, B. (2000). What makes the difference? Children and teachers talk about resilient outcomes for children 'at risk'. *Educational Studies, 26*, 321-337.

Martin, A. (2002). Motivation and academic resilience: Developing a model for student enhancement. *Australian journal of education, 46*(1), 34-49.

[17] Rath, L., Olmstead, K., Zhang, J., & Beach, P. (2019). Hearing students' voices: Understanding student perspectives of online learning. *Online Journal of Distance Learning Administration, 22*(4)

[18] Bartkus, K. R., Nemelka, B., Nemelka, M., & Gardner, P. (2012). Clarifying the meaning of extracurricular activity: a literature review of definitions. *American Journal of Business Education (AJBE), 5*(6), 693–704. https://doi.org/10.19030/ajbe.v5i6.7391

Keaton, W., & Gilbert, A. (2020). Successful Online Learning: What Does Learner Interaction with Peers, Instructors and Parents Look Like? *Journal of Online Learning Research, 6*(2), 135–136.

[19] Berry, S. (2019). Comparing and contrasting the perspectives of online students and faculty. *Online Learning, 23*(4). https://doi.org/10.24059/olj.v23i4.2038

Nicklin, L. L., Wilsdon, L., Chadwick, D., Rhoden, L., Ormerod, D., Allen, D., Witton, G., & Lloyd, J. (2022). Accelerated HE digitalization: Exploring staff and student experiences of the COVID-19 rapid online-learning transfer. *Education and Information Technologies, 27*(6), 7653-7678. doi.org/10.1007/s10639-022- 10899-8

Snijders, I., Wijnia, L., Dekker, H. J. J., Rikers, Remy M. J. P, & Loyens, S. M. M. (2022). What is in a student-faculty relationship?: A template analysis of students' positive and negative critical incidents with faculty and staff in higher education. *European Journal of Psychology of Education, 37*(4), 1115- 1139. https://doi.org/10.1007/s10212-021-00549-x

[20] Berry, S. (2019). Comparing and contrasting the perspectives of online students and faculty. *Online Learning, 23*(4). https://doi.org/10.24059/olj.v23i4.2038

Nicklin, L. L., Wilsdon, L., Chadwick, D., Rhoden, L., Ormerod, D., Allen, D., Witton, G., & Lloyd, J. (2022). Accelerated HE digitalization: Exploring staff and student experiences of the COVID-19 rapid online-learning transfer. *Education and Information Technologies, 27*(6), 7653-7678. doi.org/10.1007/s10639-022- 10899-8

Snijders, I., Wijnia, L., Dekker, H. J. J., Rikers, Remy M. J. P, & Loyens, S. M. M. (2022). What is in a student-faculty relationship?: A template analysis of students' positive and negative critical incidents with faculty and staff in higher education. *European Journal of Psychology of Education, 37*(4), 1115- 1139. https://doi.org/10.1007/s10212-021-00549-x

[21] Hensley, L. C., Iaconelli, R., & Wolters, C. A. (2022). "this weird time we're in": How a sudden change to remote education

impacted college students' self-regulated learning. *Journal of Research on Technology in Education, 54*(S1), S203- S218. https://doi.org/10.1080/15391523.2021.1916414

[22] Felder, R. M., & Brent, R. (2004). The intellectual development of Science and engineering students. part 1: Models and challenges. *Journal of Engineering Education, 93*(4), 269–277. https://doi.org/10.1002/j.2168-9830.2004.tb00816.x

Gobec, C., Turnbull, M., & Rillotta, F. (2022). Lessons learnt from transitioning to online mentoring and learning at university during COVID-19 for adults with intellectual disability. *Journal of Intellectual Disabilities, 26*(4), 869-884.

[23] Dhanjal, R., Dine, K., Gerdts, J., Merrill, K., Frykas, T. L. M., & Protudjer, J. L. (2023). An online, peer-mentored food allergy education program improves children's and parents' confidence. *Allergy, Asthma, and Clinical Immunology, 19*(1), 47- 47. https://doi.org/10.1186/s13223-023-00800-8

Frith, K. M. (2023). *Examining adult learners' engagement in an online course*: A qualitative study.

Glyn-Jones, S. (2023). *An Ethnographic Study of 'Resurface' : a Wellbeing Intervention for University Students* (Order No. 30532225). Available from ProQuest Dissertations & Theses Global. (2810062296). Grimaldi, E., & Ball, S. J. (2021). Paradoxes of freedom. an archaeological analysis of educational online platform interfaces. *Critical Studies in Education, 62*(1), 114- 129. https://doi.org/10.1080/17508487.2020.1861043

Li, J., & Wang, R. (2023). Machine learning adoption in educational institutions: Role of internet of things and digital educational platforms. *Sustainability (Basel, Switzerland), 15*(5), 4000. https://doi.org/10.3390/su15054000

Li, L., & Huang, W. (2023). Effects of undergraduate student reviewers' ability on comments provided, reviewing behavior, and performance in an online video peer assessment activity.

Educational Technology & Society, 26(2), 76- 93. https://doi.org/10.30191/ETS.202304_26(2).0006

Li, L., Shi, J., & Zhong, B. (2023). Good in arts, good at computer? Rural students' computer skills are bolstered by arts and science literacies. *Computers in Human Behavior, 140,* 107573.

Wilson, C., Arshad, R., Sapouna, M., McGillivray, D., & Zihms, S. (2023). 'PGR connections': Using an online peer- learning pedagogy to support doctoral researchers. Innovations in Education and Teaching International, 60(3), 390- 400. https://doi.org/10.1080/14703297.2022.2141292

[24] Glyn-Jones, S. (2023). *An Ethnographic Study of 'Resurface' : a Wellbeing Intervention for University Students* (Order No. 30532225). Available from ProQuest Dissertations & Theses Global. (2810062296). Grimaldi, E., & Ball, S. J. (2021). Paradoxes of freedom. an archaeological analysis of educational online platform interfaces. *Critical Studies in Education, 62*(1), 114- 129. https://doi.org/10.1080/17508487.2020.1861043

Sadykova, G. (2014). Mediating knowledge through peer-to-peer interaction in a multicultural online learning environment: A case of international students in the US. *The International Review of Research in Open and Distributed Learning, 15*(3). https://doi.org/10.19173/irrodl.v15i3.1629

[25] Hartong, S., & Decuypere, M. (2023). Platformed professional(itie)s and the ongoing digital transformation of education. *Tertium Comparationis, 29*(1), 1–21. https://doi.org/10.31244/tc.2023.01.01

Sofi-Karim, M., Bali, A. O., & Rached, K. (2023). Online education via media platforms and applications as an innovative teaching method. *Education and Information Technologies, 28*(1), 507-523. https://doi.org/10.1007/s10639-022-11188-0

[26] He, S., Jiang, S., Zhu, R., & Hu, X. (2023). The influence of educational and emotional support on e-learning acceptance: An integration of social support theory and TAM. *Education*

and Information Technologies, 1-21. *Macmillan English dictionary for Advanced Learners*. (2007). Macmillan.

[27] Beam, A. P. (2023). Creating Meaningful Relationships in the Online Environment: Building Rapport With the Adult Learner. In *Motivation and Momentum in Adult Online Education* (pp. 18-34). IGI Global.

He, S., Jiang, S., Zhu, R., & Hu, X. (2023). The influence of educational and emotional support on e-learning acceptance: An integration of social support theory and TAM. *Education and Information Technologies*, 1-21. *Macmillan English dictionary for Advanced Learners*. (2007). Macmillan.

[28] Chen, T., Luo, H., Feng, Q., & Li, G. (2023). Effect of technology acceptance on blended learning satisfaction: The serial mediation of emotional experience, social belonging, and higher-order thinking. *International Journal of Environmental Research and Public Health*, 20(5), 4442.

[29] Morese, R. (2020). Social isolation: An interdisciplinary view. Intech Open.

Tang, K., Hsiao, C., Tu, Y., Hwang, G., & Wang, Y. (2021). Factors influencing university teachers' use of a mobile technology-enhanced teaching (MTT) platform. *Educational Technology Research and Development*, 69(5), 2705- 2728. https://doi.org/10.1007/s11423-021-10032-5

[30] Alshammari, M. K., Othman, M. H., Mydin, Y. O., & Mohammed, B. A. (2023). The Effect of Social Isolation on the Mental Health of International Students.

Dong, Y., & Ishige, A. (2022). Studying abroad from home: An exploration of international graduate students' perceptions and experiences of emergency remote teaching. *Education Sciences*, 12(2), 98. https://doi.org/10.3390/educsci12020098

Mizani, H., Cahyadi, A., Hendryadi, H., Salamah, S., & Retno Sari, S. (2022).

Loneliness, student engagement, and academic achievement during emergency remote teaching during COVID-19: The role of the god locus of control. *Humanities & Social Sciences Communications, 9*(1), 305- 305. https://doi.org/10.1057/s41599-022-01328-9

Morese, R. (2020). *Social isolation: An interdisciplinary view.* IntechOpen.

Morgan, H. (2022). Alleviating the challenges with remote learning during a pandemic. *Education Sciences, 12*(2), 109. https://doi.org/10.3390/educsci12020109

Tang, K., Hsiao, C., Tu, Y., Hwang, G., & Wang, Y. (2021). Factors influencing university teachers' use of a mobile technology-enhanced teaching (MTT) platform. *Educational Technology Research and Development, 69*(5), 2705- 2728. https://doi.org/10.1007/s11423-021-10032-5

[31] Hoi, V. N., & Le Hang, H. (2021). The structure of student engagement in online learning: A bi-factor exploratory structural equation modelling approach. *Journal of Computer Assisted Learning, 37*(4), 1141- 1153. https://doi.org/10.1111/jcal.12551

Trowler, V. (2010). Student engagement literature review. *The Higher Education Academy, 11*(1), 1-15.

[32] Hoi, V. N., & Le Hang, H. (2021). The structure of student engagement in online learning: A bi-factor exploratory structural equation modelling approach. *Journal of Computer Assisted Learning, 37*(4), 1141- 1153. https://doi.org/10.1111/jcal.12551

[33] Proverbs 27:17

[34] Luke 2:51; Heb. 5:8

[35] Luke 2:46-52

[36] Mark 6:7

CHAPTER 2 SOURCE MATERIAL

[1] https://www.history.com/news/what-was-the-shot-heard-round-the-world

[2] Brumwell, S. (2016). George Washington: Gentleman warrior. Quercus.

[3] Bergman, B., Negretti, R., Spencer-Oatey, H., & Stöhr, C. (2023). Integrating Home and International Students in HE: Academic and Social Effects of Pair Work PBL Assignments Online. Journal of Studies in International Education, 10283153221150117.

He, S., Jiang, S., Zhu, R., & Hu, X. (2023). The influence of educational and emotional support on e-learning acceptance: An integration of social support theory and TAM. Education and Information Technologies, 1-21.

[4] https://hbr.org/2022/03/the-great-resignation-didnt-start-with-the-pandemic

[5] https://hbr.org/2022/03/the-great-resignation-didnt-start-with-the-pandemic

[6] https://www.newsnationnow.com/banfield/losing-the-faith-the-great-pastor-resignation/

[7] Robinson, H., Al-Freih, M., & Kilgore, W. (2020). Designing with care. The International Journal of Information and Learning Technology, 37(3), 99–108. https://doi.org/10.1108/ijilt-10-2019-0098

Sitzman, K., & Leners, D. W., Student perceptions of caring in online baccalaureate education.

Toma, R., & Berge, M. (2023). Online Teaching in a Time of Crisis: Social Capital and Community Building Tools. International Journal of Advanced Corporate Learning, 16(1), 65.

Velasquez, A., Graham, C. R., & Osguthorpe, R. (2013). Caring in a technology- mediated online high school context. Distance Education, 34(1), 97–118. https://doi.org/10.1080/01587919.2013.770435

[8]   Arbaugh, J. B. (2001). How instructor immediacy behaviors affect student satisfaction and learning in web-based courses. Business Communication Quarterly, 64(4), 42-54.

Jaggars, S. S., & Xu, D. (2016). How do online course design features influence student performance?. Computers & Education, 95, 270-284.

Means, B., Bakia, M., & Murphy, R. (2014). Learning online: What research tells us about whether, when and how. Routledge.

Picciano, A. G. (2002). Beyond student perceptions: Issues of interaction, presence, and performance in an online course. Journal of Asynchronous learning networks, 6(1), 21-40.

Tate, T., & Warschauer, M. (2022). Equity in online learning. Educational Psychologist, 57(3), 192-206.

[9]   George, A., McEwan, A., & Tarr, J. (2021). Accountability in educational dialogue on attrition rates: Understanding external attrition factors and isolation in online law school. Australasian Journal of Educational Technology, 37(1), 111- 132. https://doi.org/10.14742/ajet.6175

Hehir, E., Zeller, M., Luckhurst, J., & Chandler, T. (2021). Developing student connectedness under remote learning using digital resources: A systematic review. Education and Information Technologies, 26(5), 6531- 6548. doi.org/10.1007/s10639-021-10577-1

Leal Filho, W., Wall, T., Rayman-Bacchus, L., Mifsud, M., Pritchard, D. J., Lovren, V. O., Farinha, C., Petrovic, D. S., & Balogun, A.-L. (2021). Impacts of covid-19 and social isolation on academic staff and students at universities: A cross- sectional study. BMC Public Health, 21(1). https://doi. org/10.1186/s12889-021- 11040-z

[10] George, A., McEwan, A., & Tarr, J. (2021). Accountability in educational dialogue on attrition rates: Understanding external attrition factors and isolation in online law school. Australasian Journal of Educational Technology, 37(1), 111- 132. https://doi. org/10.14742/ajet.6175

Hehir, E., Zeller, M., Luckhurst, J., & Chandler, T. (2021). Developing student connectedness under remote learning using digital resources: A systematic review. Education and Information Technologies, 26(5), 6531- 6548. doi.org/10.1007/ s10639-021-10577-1

Leal Filho, W., Wall, T., Rayman-Bacchus, L., Mifsud, M., Pritchard, D. J., Lovren, V. O., Farinha, C., Petrovic, D. S., & Balogun, A.-L. (2021). Impacts of covid-19 and social isolation on academic staff and students at universities: A cross- sectional study. BMC Public Health, 21(1). https://doi. org/10.1186/s12889-021- 11040-z

[11] Robinson, H., Al-Freih, M., & Kilgore, W. (2020). Designing with care. The International Journal of Information and Learning Technology, 37(3), 99–108. https://doi.org/10.1108/ ijilt-10-2019-0098

Sitzman, K., & Leners, D. W., Student perceptions of caring in online baccalaureate education. Nursing education perspectives. https://pubmed.ncbi.nlm.nih.gov/17036683/

Toma, R., & Berge, M. (2023). Online Teaching in a Time of Crisis: Social Capital and Community Building Tools. International Journal of Advanced Corporate Learning, 16(1), 65.

Velasquez, A., Graham, C. R., & Osguthorpe, R. (2013). Caring in a technology- mediated online high school context. Distance Education, 34(1), 97–118. https://doi.org/10.1080/01587919.20 13.770435

[12]   Mizani, H., Cahyadi, A., Hendryadi, H., Salamah, S., & Retno Sari, S. (2022). Loneliness, student engagement, and academic achievement during emergency remote teaching during COVID-19: The role of the god locus of control. Humanities & Social Sciences Communications, 9(1), 305- 305. https://doi.org/10.1057/s41599-022-01328-9

Morese, R. (2020). Social isolation: An interdisciplinary view. IntechOpen.

Umoh, M. E., Prichett, L., Boyd, C. M., & Cudjoe, T. K. (2023). Impact of technology on social isolation: Longitudinal analysis from the National Health Aging Trends Study. Journal of the American Geriatrics Society, 71(4), 1117- 1123.

[13]   Greenland, S. J., & Moore, C. (2022). Large qualitative sample and thematic analysis to redefine student dropout and retention strategy in open online education. British Journal of Educational Technology, 53(3), 647-667.

Luo, N., Li, H., Zhao, L., Wu, Z., & Zhang, J. (2022). Promoting student engagement in online learning through harmonious classroom environment. The Asia-Pacific Education Researcher, 31(5), 541-551.

Versteeg, M., Kappe, R. F., & Knuiman, C. (2022). Predicting student engagement: the role of academic belonging, social integration, and resilience during COVID-19 emergency remote teaching. Frontiers in Public Health, 10, 849594.

[14]   https://www.insidehighered.com/news/2020/04/20/new-report-says-many-adjuncts-make- less-3500-course-and-25000-year

[15]   Oducado, R. M. F., Amboy, M. K. Q., Penuela, A. C., Dela Rosa, R. D., Fajardo, M. T. M., & Temelo, D. R. F. (2022). Instructors' caring behaviors, burnout, satisfaction, and academic performance of nursing students in online education and the pandemic era. Frontiers of Nursing, 9(4), 431- 437. https://doi.org/10.2478/fon-2022-0054

Park, S., & Robinson, P. A. (2022). The effect of online academic coaches on supporting graduate students' performance in intensive online learning environments: A three- course comparison. European Journal of Training and Development, 46(1/2), 70-85. https://doi.org/10.1108/EJTD-10-2020-0144

Sotardi, V. A. (2022). On institutional belongingness and academic performance: Mediating effects of social self-efficacy and metacognitive strategies. Studies in Higher Education, 47(12), 2444–2459. https://doi.org/10.1080/03075079.2022.2081678

[16] Chen, D. (2022). Application of IoT-oriented online education platform in english teaching. Mathematical Problems in Engineering, 2022, 1- 9. https://doi.org/10.1155/2022/9606706

Erdem-Aydin, İ. (2021). Investigation of higher education instructors' perspectives towards emergency remote teaching. Educational Media International, 58(1), 78- 98. https://doi.org/10.1080/09523987.2021.1908501

CHAPTER 3 SOURCE MATERIAL

[1]   https://olympics.com/en/athletes/jesse-owens

[2]   https://www.olympedia.org/athletes/51028

[3]   https://www.defense.gov/News/Feature-Stories/story/Article/ 2304075/sports-heroes-who-served-olympic-runner-louis- zamperini/

[4]   https://www.history.com/this-day-in-history/hitler-oversees- 1936-berlin-olympics

[5]   Brown, D. J. (2023). The boys in the boat: Nine Americans and their epic quest for gold at the 1936 Berlin Olympics. Penguin Books. https://www.youtube.com/watch?v=lK8S3wgmDEA

[6]   Brown, D. J. (2023). The boys in the boat: Nine Americans and their epic quest for gold at the 1936 Berlin Olympics. Penguin Books. https://www.youtube.com/watch?v=lK8S3wgmDEA

[7]   (Ferri, 2020; Lambert, 2020 & Scherer, 2021).

CHAPTER 4 SOURCE MATERIAL

[1]   Wildfire Today - news and opinion about wildland fire. (n.d.). https://
        wildfiretoday.com/documents/AnalysisDodgeEscapeFireon
        1949MannGulchFireSurvivalZone.pdf

[2]   Useem, M. (2000). The leadership moment: Nine true stories of
        triumph and disaster and their lessons for us all. Three Rivers
        Press.

[3]   Useem, M. (2000). The leadership moment: Nine true stories of
        triumph and disaster and their lessons for us all. Three Rivers
        Press.

CHAPTER 5 SOURCE MATERIAL

[1]   McCullough, The Wright Brothers

Dec. 17, 1903: Wright Brothers take flight at NC's Outer Banks ... (n.d.). https://www.13newsnow.com/article/news/history/dec-17-1903-wright-brothers-take-flight-at-ncs-outer-banks/291-555a6b6d-9c69-4427-b270-b7a7f6ad92ab

The Wright Brothers at Kitty Hawk. Homepage. (n.d.). https://airandspace.si.edu/stories/editorial/wright-brothers-kitty-hawk

Thomas, E. (2021, December 17). *Breakdown: Why the Wright brother's chose the city of Kitty Hawk for their first flight.* https://www.actionnews5.com. https://www.actionnews5.com/2021/12/17/breakdown-why-wright-brothers-chose-city-kitty-hawk-their-first-flight/

U.S. Department of the Interior. (n.d.). *Commemorating the wright brothers at Kitty Hawk (U.S. National Park Service).* National Parks Service. https://www.nps.gov/articles/commemoration.htm

CHAPTER 6 SOURCE MATERIAL

[1] Alfred Lansing. Endurance: Shackleton's Incredible Voyage (Kindle Locations 234-235). Kindle Edition.

[2] (Rath et al., 2019 & Van Wart et al., 2020).

[3] (Alias, 2005 & Fibriasari et al., 2023)

[4] (Alias, 2005 & Fibriasari et al., 2023).

[5] (Chen et al., 2023)

[6] (Tinto, 1975, 1993, 2022).

[7] (Hehir, 2021 & Winters et al., 2023).

[8] Alfred Lansing. Endurance: Shackleton's Incredible Voyage (Kindle Locations 103-104). Kindle Edition.

[9] (Berry, 2019; Kranzow, 2013; Nicklin et al., 2022 & Snijders et al., 2022).

[10] (Sopina, 2015 & Watkins et al., 2014)

[11] (Chickering, 1989 & Tan et al., 2021).

[12] George E. Marston (1882-1940) - biographical notes. George E. Marston (1882-1940) Biographical notes. (n.d.). https://www.coolantarctica.com/Antarctica%20fact%20file/History/biography/marston_g eorge.php

[13] Alfred Lansing. Endurance: Shackleton's Incredible Voyage (Kindle Locations 234-235). Kindle Edition.

[14] Tyler-Lewis, Kelly. The Lost Men: The Harrowing Saga of Shackleton's Ross Sea Party. Penguin Publishing Group. Kindle Edition.

[15] (Lambert, 2020).

[16] (Abduraxmanova, 2022 & Lakhal et al., 2020).

CHAPTER 7 SOURCE MATERIAL

[1]   Aitken, Jonathan. John Newton (Foreword by Philip Yancey): From Disgrace to Amazing Grace (p. 18). Crossway. Kindle Edition.

[2]   Aitken, Jonathan. John Newton (Foreword by Philip Yancey): From Disgrace to Amazing Grace (p. 78). Crossway. Kindle Edition.

[3]   Aitken, Jonathan. John Newton (Foreword by Philip Yancey): From Disgrace to Amazing Grace (p. 97). Crossway. Kindle Edition.

[4]   Aitken, Jonathan. John Newton (Foreword by Philip Yancey): From Disgrace to Amazing Grace (p. 351). Crossway. Kindle Edition.

[5]   Aitken, Jonathan. John Newton (Foreword by Philip Yancey): From Disgrace to Amazing Grace (p. 171). Crossway. Kindle Edition.

[6]   Aitken, Jonathan. John Newton (Foreword by Philip Yancey): From Disgrace to Amazing Grace (p. 351). Crossway. Kindle Edition.

[7]   Aitken, Jonathan. John Newton (Foreword by Philip Yancey): From Disgrace to Amazing Grace (p. 351). Crossway. Kindle Edition.

ABOUT THE AUTHOR

Dr. Daniel Day is a passionate follower of Jesus Christ, husband, father, local church pastor, educator, and consultant. Dr. Day holds a Master's in Christian Leadership from the University of Valley Forge and a Ph.D. in Education & Organizational Leadership from Liberty University. He enjoys building things from the ground up, as well as working with teams to breathe new life into their organization. Most of all, Dr. Day enjoys assisting people in their journey to become all that God has called them to be and investing in the lives of the next generation.

ABOUT THE BOOK

After ten years of online education, I had earned an MA and a Ph.D. Though incredibly grateful for this time of learning and growing, there was still something amiss once it was all finished. It wasn't easy to figure out why I felt this way, but it finally came to me. Ultimately, I cannot point to one meaningful long-term friendship that was formed with either a peer or professor. The accessible, convenient, and affordable pathways of online educational delivery systems paved the way for me to achieve my learning goals, and for that, I am thankful. Yet, the feeling of being robbed of the human element and the benefit of gaining another's perspective remained.

Online education is here to stay. No one is arguing that fact. Even now, new technological advancements continue to emerge, offering innovative approaches to helping people to continue learning. I celebrate this and encourage it, but not at the expense of the human element. This book puts forward research-based findings that offer evidence that students, professors, and schools are far more likely to achieve their goals when solid friendships exist.

A solidly Christian and Biblical perspective undergirds and supports the results of this one-and-a-half-year doctoral research project that is the basis for this book. Questions that are considered through these pages include:

1. Why do relationships matter in online education?
2. Who is responsible for creating relational connections in online education?

3. Where and when can social opportunities happen in online education?
4. Is there a Biblical precedent for learning in relational communities?
5. Are there dangers to learning in isolation?

By using inspirational true stories, Biblical examples, and data gleaned from the research, arguments are made that all in online education win if genuine friendships exist, and we enjoy the support of a Christian community.

FURTHER RESOURCES

To download a free copy of the doctoral dissertation which serves as the foundation for this book, visit
https://digitalcommons.liberty.edu/doctoral/5246/

Also, by Daniel Day
STOKED: 7 Strategies for Kindling & Keeping Your Fire for God While in Christian College